Hearing Inner Voices: The Dead Pet Whisperer

By
Linda J. Brown

Copyright © 2016 by Linda J. Brown

All rights reserved.

Book design by Linda J. Brown

No part of this book may be reproduced in any form or by any electronic or mechanical means including information storage and retrieval systems, without permission in writing from the author. The only exception is by a reviewer, who may quote short excerpts in a review.

Linda J. Brown Books are available for order through Ingram Press Catalogues

Visit my website at www.insecretdiffusion.com

Printed in the United States of America
First Printing: 2016
Published by Sojourn Publishing, LLC

ISBN: 978-0-9820049-4-4

DEDICATION

To every courageous Earthling who has ever "Heard Voices" within their own head and who has decided to answer back, willing to carry on an Inner Conversation.

To every sweet animal who has ever come to the surface of Planet Earth, willing to become a family member of the Human Race. To love, to teach, and to lead a shorter life.

To every reader longing to ask Cosmic Questions and to learn more and more about Life, Death, and the Universe.

ACKNOWLEDGEMENTS

This book could not have been written without the numerous and probing questions which readers have posted on my Metaphysical website, www.insecretdiffusion.com, which solicits cosmic questions from the public.

Over the past five years, people have written to me with their wonderment about life's puzzles. Naturally, a great many of those include questions about death, especially when it happens to their beloved pets. The general public has much information in our available literature to comfort survivors concerning **human** continuation after death; but very little, if any, about an **animal's** soul survival. The subject usually doesn't occur to us until our heart is ripped open by the departure of a loved creature, whose life and happiness has always been in our hands. "Are they all right?" is the most common question I hear. The good news of the continued existence and awaiting reunion of every Little Darling usually helps that grieving human to regain their emotional balance and go on living.

All subjects listed herein have been submitted by readers of my blog. My appreciation goes to every one of them for writing in, because the truth is, that until a question is posed, there can be no succinct answer. I never know what I'm going to receive when I take Dictation on any topic. Much is quite surprising!

Also, if Voice Hearers ignore or squelch their sometimes-alarming talent; such experiences can never be accessed and publically-shared. So, my second acknowledgement goes to the Voice Hearers of the World, who are finally coming out of their closets and organizing themselves into networks. Thus, they can compare notes and encourage each other, while enabling professional scientists to have a look at this strange phenomenon, which is, only now, becoming seriously studied for what it is. As I embark upon my third, solo, around-the-world exploration, I intend to visit the Hearing Voices Networks and the universities where this ground-breaking research on

Clairaudience is taking place. I will do whatever I can to advance this knowledge.

You are welcome to visit my two websites: www.heyboomers.com and www.insecretdiffusion.com, as well as to read my three other published books found on Amazon.com.

Thanks also to my own darling granddaughter Molly, my cover model.

CONTENTS

Dedication iii
Acknowledgements v
Introduction xi

CHAPTER ONE – THE DEAD PETS' SOCIETY 1
Most Surviving Pet Owners 1
How Your Dead Dog Feels When You Cry 2
A Bereaved Pet Owner 3
A Meeting Place For Others 6
Why We Can't Feel Our Dead Beloveds 7
A Spaniel's Death And His Owner's Vision Of Him 10
Do Pets Reincarnate And Choose Their Owners? 18
Pets Can Choose To Reincarnate 20
How Do You Live With Euthanizing Your Pet? 24
The Death Of Your Pet Teaches You Detachment 28
Even The Death Of A Tiny Pet Leaves Big Holes 29
A Message From A Ferret 35
How Would I Know If My Dead Gram Is Near? 37
Do Humans Reincarnate As Animals? Pets As Humans? 41

CHAPTER TWO–THE NEW MILLENNIUM AND VOICE HEARING 43
Hearing Your Inner Voice And Answering It 43
Time Is An Environment 51
The Origin Of The God Consciousness, And Why Not A Female God? 55

News Flash! God Both Does And Doesn't Exist! 57
In What Dimension Is The Holy Spirit Who Speaks
To Me? 59

CHAPTER THREE–HUMAN CHARACTERISTICS 61
Heaven's Opinion Of Happiness 61
In Defense Of Ridiculously Silly Human Beings 63
God's Own Ability To Speak Directly To Humans 65
Where Do Our Prayers Go? What Do They Do? 67
Prayer Feels This Way From The Other Side 70
Is A Heavy-Matter Realm Important To Spiritualization? 71
Among Differing Psychic Information,
Which Can We Trust? 73
Are Psychic Talents Alien To Planet Earth? 76
How In The Hell Did I Get Here? 78
Is Possession Real? 80
Could Consciousness Also Be A Magnetic Force? 81
Is Modern Technology Changing Consciousness? 83
Why Do Humans Have A Hunger To Find A Mate? 86
Developing Inner Hearing Abilities 89
How Can Mankind Develop A New Cosmic Consciousness? 91
Are Human Lives Scripted? 97
Can People With Different Backgrounds Get Along? 99
Human fear–of snakes and otherwise 101
Is There A Fear Eliminator? 103
How Does Bone-Jarring, Window-Rattling Music Affect
Its Regular Listeners? 104
Any Comments For The Atheists And Agnostics? 108

What Are Acid-Based Protozoa?..109
Achieving Humanity's Overall Benefit 112

CHAPTER FOUR–STARSEEDS 115
Commander Ashtar Sheran Of The Intergalactic Federation 115
Orion's and Pleiades' Effect On The Earth's Population?........120
A Conversation About Orion Starseeds.................................122
Does Being A Starseed Go Against God?.................................125

CHAPTER FIVE–THE SOUL AND HUMAN DEATH, BIRTH AND LIFE, ITSELF..129
What Does The Term "Spiritualized" Really Mean? 129
Which Chakra Are You Working Out Of?..................................130
What Happens When We Fight Death? 133
What Does Déjà Vu Tell Us About Our Life? 135
A Full, Effective and Practical Guide To Communicating With The Holy Spirit..138
Setting Out Upon God's Good Sea...140
Dream Advice To Potential Suicides 141
Do You Have An Earwig Singing In Your Head? 144
In Changing Dimensions Between Life And Death................146
Death And Butterflies 150
Does The Presence Of A Soul Provide Vital Energy? 152
Heaven And Hell...153
The Hallmark Of Negative Behavior Is Elimination 154
How Do The Dead React When Heaven Is Different From Their Expectations? 155
Why Some Departed Souls Can't Communicate 157

About The Fear Of Death 158
Do We Always Reincarnate To The Same Planet? 159
Life Is Like The Tossing Of Grains Of Sand 160

CHAPTER SIX–THE VOICE-HEARING PHENOMENON 163
How My Own Inner Voices Started 163
My Co-Author, The Holy Spirit 167
My First Memory Of Speaking To The Air 172
How My Life Developed As A Silent Psychic 181
What Does It Feel Like And What Are The Risks? 182
Why Did This Unusual Experience Happen To Me? 190
A Fable – Part One to Part Four 192
Present Day 194
References 197
About The Author 199

INTRODUCTION

Hearing Inner Voices – or some version of receiving knowledge from Above, such as sudden, unexplained Knowings, Visions, or Sounds – has always been reported by a few, rare individuals. But, in our time, the decades around the Year 2000 have been filled with more and more confessed Voice Hearers. "Normal" people suddenly report that their inner channels have opened. Some children are even born with these talents in full operation, and may have unseen playmates and companions. Traditionally, such psychic children have been trained out of their fantasies by the time they reach adulthood, squelching and denying their unusual birthright.

At last, Voice Hearing Networks are making it possible for all sorts of closeted psychic ones to share stories and compare notes. A movement, with early roots in the 1990s, has become a robust society in England, where there are now well over two-hundred active groups. By contrast, the United States has far fewer formally-organized Voice Hearing groups. Let us help that statistic to change – because this movement will enable all to progress beyond Psychiatry's kneejerk opinions. In fact, the most vocal members of these societies in the UK are not endowed with mysterious talents. They are medical professionals who have observed that this isn't always crazy behavior. But, what are we? Scientists are now requesting our help to get to the root of that new question. My first stop will be Durham University in Durham, UK, which has become the Center For The Study Of Hearing Inner Voices. Contact: Hearing The Voice, c/o School of Education, Durham University, Leazes Rd., Durham, DH11SZ. +44(0)1913348163 Dr. Charles Fernyhough & Dr. Angela Woods.

In fact, as most of us have discovered, it's only personal fear or alarm that causes such frantic behavior on our part to end this odd, "Upper-Realm" form of communication. Much of the need to deny our metaphysical component is the work of family and friends, who simply want us to get back to normal. So, a new opportunity has recently presented itself to understand our own situation, and to assist those scientists who are now taking a closer look at the many forms of this wondrous reality. I encourage all Voice Hearers to speak up about their own experiences.

I became a Hearer, very suddenly, at age forty-two, and I immediately felt the downside caused by this misunderstood mental state among the uninformed public. Today's surge of curiosity can only be attributed to a growing crowd of perfectly sane Voice Hearers– and I'm so grateful for this opportunity to share my own conclusions, gathered over the past thirty-five years. By this time, I have published one book on the subject: *In Secret Diffusion: The Upper Realm Answers Questions About Earth*. I have also run my metaphysical website of the same name for the past four years, soliciting questions from the public to ask The Holy Spirit. Selected questions and answers from that site make up this book, along with a brief story about my own hearing channel and its opening.

During more than three decades, I have been in deep conversation with The Holy Spirit, Who comes to me every moment that I turn my mind towards Him. I've always been free to ask questions about mankind's presence and purpose on Earth. When I ran out of my own questions, which were contained in my first book, I created the website www.insecretdiffusion.com, where the public is free to ask theirs. Some of those appear within this book.

These explanations are not meant to be anything but a free sharing of information, and they certainly don't pretend to be the final word. They are definitely not edicts or commands from On High, but are simply comments about subjects we can all find interesting. You are welcome to pose your questions concerning the nature of our various planes of existence.

My challenge in writing this book has been to balance the various voices so that you can easily sort out the speakers. When asking my own questions, I'll usually type those in Italics and put His answer within quotation marks in regular print. This can be confusing if a third voice chimes in, such as one of the dead pets, or even a new comment by the person submitting a question through me. Also, being blog posts, they were each written on different dates throughout many countries as I traveled around the world. Then, they became scrambled when I sorted them into subject matter. Please forgive this rather colorful detail, if you can. I don't believe that it interferes with the timeless logic of the answer given.

I realize how annoying capitalized words in the middle of sentences can be. There are many here because my subject refers to matters of a different dimension mixing with our Earth affairs. Capitals help to sort out those topics or speakers connected with the Invisible Realms.

By far, the most recurring subject on my public website, where I answer any question without charge, has been the one concerning the death of animals. Some pet owners need reassurance when they lose a precious animal and can't find information about whether they survive death. My website comes up when they Google the subject, and they eagerly write their questions, so relieved to find somebody willing to tackle this topic. Thus, I've dedicated this book to a fictional "Dead Pets" Society, in the hopes that a few pet-loving humans can avoid agony when their beloved furry children leave them far too soon. Many spiritual teachings explain that man survives death, although as individuals, we don't universally accept that truth. These inner reports, that I have received, say basically the same thing. There is a certain difference, to be sure – because an animal's purpose in coming to Earth may not be the same as ours.

Pet owners fall into two categories, in my estimation. Most of us are fairly casual about the shorter life span of our dear animals. Others experience such a deep love for their pet that they treat its death like an emergency situation, similar to a tragic loss which they must, somehow, rectify. Because they have no spiritual assurances, and perhaps not even a belief in their own continuation, they unreasonably feel that they must rescue their beloved lost animal. Meanwhile, as with grief in general, they seek some way to calm themselves down.

So, even if this isn't the most scholarly or virtuous of topics to be sought by a questioner, it's apparently the most relevant and probably the most urgently needed.

I don't pretend or claim to be a psychic. I really solicit only general cosmic questions that are applicable to all, and I don't answer those queries wanting contact with a particular person on the Other Side. But, who can resist an answer from a particular pet? So, I make my exceptions. Besides, as you'll see, some animals are fond of puns and can give some cute, wry little answers in the process of comforting their grieving owners.

CHAPTER ONE
THE DEAD PETS' SOCIETY

MOST SURVIVING PET OWNERS ARE IN MUCH WORSE SHAPE THAN THEIR DEAD PETS

Naza writes:

"I recently lost my dog. He was the one person I was closest to. I just want to know if he's happy where he is, if he has anything he wants to tell me and if he's going to ever come back to me like I asked him to, several times, before he passed. I don't know if it's wrong or right for me to go out and get a new puppy. I don't know if he wants to come back, but my heart aches for him. Please help me! Please!"

Oh my Holy Spirit! What do You have to say to this bereaved pet owner?

"Oh My God, Linda Layli! This is a typical feeling of owners who have lost their beloved. It is a statement of unity among them, and they all feel exactly the same emotions – especially that of being disloyal by getting another dog to replace that best friend. If they could only think straight for a moment, they would be able to understand what's going on here. Animals don't live as long as humans do. The only way to avoid this dilemma is not to own a pet in the first place. And, for this sort of an animal lover, that is not an option.

So, Naza, of course you will always be Best Friends. Luckily, this isn't doled out to you as a once-in-a-lifetime occurrence. Since death doesn't really exist for any sentient being – it's simply a movement into a new condition – you will be reunited in the future. Get over this grief as best you can! These pets are just fine in their new home, Up Here, with Me! In fact, they're in a much better place than you occupy. Please don't call them to regress back into your Earth Level where they sacrifice so much to fit into their role.

Death is a shock to people left behind on Earth, but it never is for the one who goes through that door. Those myths about it are strangely true. No matter how much people fear death, the truth is different from what you might think.

I can't tell you whether to start over again with another animal. It's neither wrong nor right. But, you might wait until these emotions subside before taking on a new personality, who deserves to be received without any lingering conditions or expectations. Live with yourself and become a little bit more independent of such emotional support before diving into a new circumstance to which you may have attached hidden strings."

Naza, you are very definitely not alone in your feelings! However, there are not as many resources to teach us about animals in the next world as there are about human spiritual survival after death. I advise you to scroll down through these blog subjects, written over the past four years, and read all that pertain to this question. You'll get a much more complete picture of what your darling pet is doing right now, and I'm sure that it will make you feel much better.

They can still be around you, but your grief can make it impossible for you to know that. Plus, if you don't have open psychic channels that are able to pick up on such subtle sensations – and this is true of most people – then you won't perceive their presence, anyway.

So, don't worry about it. Live your life, simply knowing that such powerful ties of love are never lost and that you will see them again "In the Sweet By and By!"

HOW YOUR DEAD DOG FEELS WHEN YOU CRY

Vilune writes: "My dog, Moly, passed away five weeks ago. She was thirteen years old. I am desperate. I can't cope with grief, and nobody can comfort me.... Please, help me to deal with this great loss. I am losing my mind...."

Oh my Holy Spirit! Do You have any words of comfort for this dear pet lover, whose dog died last month?

"Oh, My God! I have this precious bundle yapping at Me to deliver the good news of its survival of death. I shall translate for Moly:

"Every single thing that you have ever read is true, is true, is true! There is a Heaven here and I have come, specifically, to urge you to settle down for my sake. When you cry, it's like you are calling me to live with you again. I can't help it that I died! I was old enough to climb Up Here, wasn't I? It seems to me that I deserve a rest!

But, I feel sad when you are sad... just like always!

You will see me again when you get Up Here, so please don't lose your mind or I will have to fetch it back to you and I'd rather not.

Just be patient with me for leaving you alone... for running away from you. I didn't mean to, but I couldn't refuse to die. You'll find out someday, too; and then we can have a nice, long bark about it.

So, cheer up and I'll see you when you arrive on This Side. It's really super-duper! Whatever you do, "Don't give up the ship!"

This is your new training course! Shall I put you through your paces, or are you going to learn to heal?"

A BEREAVED PET OWNER, RECOVERING FROM THE DEATH OF HIS PRECIOUS YORKIE DOG

Ray writes:

I have spent the past month since Flori, my darling, young Yorkshire Terrier passed over. At sixty-four years of age, I can testify that within the few glorious months we spent on this

Earthly plane, Flori taught me more about love than any other of my varied life experiences did. I must thank this article for giving me some ease that Flori is well. For you see, so wonderful was our love, that if I knew for sure that Flori was unhappy and wanted me to come to her now, I would go to her.

So I close, with many thanks, and wonder how I may get to know if Flori wants me to have another dog, and/or just what are her wishes?

God bless you all – Ray

Oh my Holy Spirit, there is often a great well of pain and sorrow out here in the world over the loss of a beloved pet. At such times, we humans have coped without the comfort and understanding, such as religion has provided, concerning the continuation of the Human Soul after death. The idea of an Animal Soul is foreign to most people; though pet owners do suspect that such exists because they witness it daily while their noble one is alive.

Even without speech, an animal can convey thoughts and deeds of such love and loyalty – often of a quality that humans simply don't find in each other. How fortunate is the Earthling who has deserved the love of an animal! Yet, common knowledge often discounts this great bond, or passes it off to mere sentimentality. That deeper level of devotion isn't granted to everyone who simply feeds and shelters.

This is the third inquiry that we've received from a pet owner who has been completely undone by the death of a beloved dog. How many millions of broken hearts do these three individuals represent? What else can we tell them besides the delightful news that their sweetheart awaits their own arrival in the Next World and still accompanies them, even now, in spirit form with no change in eternal devotion? Ray asks:

1. How can he possibly replace his Flori with another dog?

2. He is willing to arrange his own death if he thought that Flori needed him Over There.
What can You say to him, oh my Holy Spirit?
"I love these sincere, loving questions. I have so many pets, Up Here, wanting to send this answer out to their owners. Oh, how they want to lick away the pain! Tell this man that whatever puppy he might choose to bring into his heart and his home will come with all of Flori's love attached to it.

There is no competition in this business of pet love; just as there is no competition within a parent's heart concerning each one of their children. Love at Ground Zero is pure and untainted. Here's what your dear, sweet Flori wants you to know, Ray:

She has taught you how to love in this degree and she certainly wants you to keep on perfecting that exuberant quality. Why don't you go on a bit of a Puppy Hunt? Let Flori choose the right little ball of fur for you. Your instincts will probably vary until you discern the exact one that she has chosen. Make a game out of it... as if this new pup is a stuffed toy that she has hidden for you to find. Talk to her all you want, the way you always have, and don't be surprised if she answers you back.

Now, her *'Woof-woof; woof-woof; woof-woof'* might make a lot more sense!

That last statement is a direct quote from your Flori, herself, just now. Love and Playfulness are very much connected. Don't let all of Flori's lessons go up in smoke. She wants you to keep on practicing those talents, and she has even more to teach as you raise a playful new puppy dog.

As to your generous, but totally undoglike suggestion that you attack yourself, in order to appear, like something the cat dragged in, upon her doorstep: she barks a sharp order to *"Fuhgeddaboudit!"* Go take somebody for a walk, instead! She will see you... and any troops that might be tagging along by that time... when the Universe whistles for you and is good and ready to receive you...and not a minute before!

"*Sit, Boy!*

Stay!
But, DON'T rollover!"

A MEETING PLACE FOR OTHERS WHO WONDER ABOUT LIFE AFTER DEATH FOR THEIR PETS

Ray's new comment:

Hi All,
First, may all you bereaved owners have found some peace! I know that for me one turning point was when I read these words: *"Blessed are the grieved for they WILL be comforted!!!* From the moment I read that, my almost-constant tears turned to random times. And, within a week of reading this, my tears have one special day of the week. Well, I still haven't fully accepted that Flori, my passed-over, Heavenly Yorkie girl, is by my side at all times in spirit. Should anyone know how, or if, I can enhance that, please post.

Well, I was given a miniature Yorkie a few weeks back. Fi-fi is very, very cute, very timid and very funny. However, I could not manage to bond with her. In fact, I think I kept myself from that, at the time, in fear of another loss. So, as my eldest daughter and her partner were looking for a companion for their Cockapoo, who Fi-fi loved to play and cuddle with, I gave her to them. Even that gift of spirit created a few tears, as I felt I had let her down. And, more than that, I had refused a gift from God???

Also, after letting Fi-fi go, I have realized my heart does have the capacity to do my best to give that pure love back to another canine, so I'm on the lookout again. To have such an effect on humans – to be able to get on heart-to-heart terms and to be blessed with the gift of understanding dogs on a deep level – is the best feeling that I have ever known.

Love like that can only come from God!

So my friends, if your canine friend has a little accident in the home, don't admonish them sternly. And, if they dawdle, when walking out, please don't keep saying *"Come on! Come on!!!"*

Be patient!!! Because that's what God is trying to say to you! Your dog is telling you that you are short on patience. This, in itself, is a gift to be nurtured.

God bless you all, canine, feline, all sentient beings! Thank you for being here!

Love, Ray

Oh my Holy Spirit! Ray has written several times since little Flori died. Is there anything You would like to say to this wonderful letter?

"Oh My God! This is the best thing you could ever say to Me! Here is what life on Earth is all about! These animals are here to teach exactly this and Ray is learning this truth so perfectly and so sincerely.

He will become the human teacher for this message, which his dear dog, Flori, brought to him. It's as if she has now gained a voice into the human world. She passed on because how could Ray have learned this precious lesson any other way?

Don't worry, Ray, whether you can feel her presence, or not. Maybe you should forget about that point and just relax. It doesn't matter to her because her presence doesn't depend upon your awareness. It's free!

She doesn't mind if you forget her...but she knows you won't. She has accomplished her mission in life and now she gets to relax. So, it's all okay. Thanks for writing in again!"

WHY WE CAN'T "FEEL" OUR DEAD BELOVEDS

Pondering Ray's last comment, I suddenly saw that it's a total blessing that he can't sense his departed pet's presence in a tangible way. The same would go for any loved one, human or animal, who may hover near a griever. Here's the reason that we should say a prayer of thanks for that merciful protection:

Because of my own long history of Inner talking with all sorts of disembodied visitors, who have passed through my days since my hearing channels opened, I can categorically say that none of them exhibit the psychic energy for me to literally "feel" their presence. I hear their voices and react by think-talking to them, privately. This way, I can relate normally to the outside world, at all times.

The very few times that I've ever localized them within my space (and I'm not sure how that worked, as it was neither sight nor sense), I have automatically changed in my behavior. I began to speak out loud and to use hand gestures while addressing them, as I would do to a living being. I tried not to bump into them or to shut a door before they came through. It's a normal human reaction to adapt to their sensed presence, though no one else can see them. Nor can I.

Ray, if you could see and sense Flori with you, then you would revert back to pet ownership of her. You would "talk to the air" or tell people, "Don't sit in that chair! She's in it!" In other words, you would go into madness, as far as this world is concerned. There's no need for that. You are here. She is there. For awhile. You are not absent from each other's thoughts, and your strong feelings, literally, pull her to you.

This is fine – but you and she are in different dimensions right now, and we, on Earth, are protected from crossing that barrier while still in the body. It's a great favor to us, because we can focus on living instead of tipping over into mental dissociation. This is why you can't feel her with you, and that's as it should be. What else is Faith about, but trusting in The Unseen? Think of how much closer to God you have become because of Flori's death. Just as you say, she's quite a teacher. So, relax on the Seeing bit. You really wouldn't want it.

When I share tips from my own personal experience, about when my Inner hearing channels "powed" open, it's important for me to remember that what happened in my case, is not, necessarily, going on within you. An infinite variety of expressions lead us along our own, individual, mystic paths. But all of these paths lead to the same place, and we fellow travelers, can, and do, share helpful tips. Right now in my own development, I realize that I'm accompanied and surrounded by those with Whom I communicate. But, I sure wouldn't want to actually SEE Them! Please understand that this is coming from a Clairaudient who doesn't "see" anything, Innerly. Maybe a Clairvoyant makes peace with the fact that dozens are right there in the shower with her. But, I haven't grown to that level yet.

Oh my Holy Spirit! What's Your take on this subject of Sensing or Seeing a disembodied Being in our own physical presence?

"It is not supposed to be happening to the living humans on Earth. They are supposed to remain ignorant of people in the next world, and their close associations with every human life. This would be like checking the inside of a watch and trying to tell what time it is. Humans are only given the power to see the clock face and not the mechanism that makes it keep time. Whenever that veil is stripped away, the one on the human level is shaken quite seriously – especially because no one else can see through that veil, and they quickly dismiss the Seer as falling into madness. Not much is gained by these glimpses of the complexity that underlies the everyday. And this is why most humans cannot penetrate these mysteries until they leave the Earth Plane.

Beloved angels do surround them, and the glue that love creates is very potent. But, both sides are free to do their work when they don't have to interrelate in their former Earthly way. Dear Flori has now become more than a simple animal who is your pet. But, if you could feel her in your presence, both of you would take up those old familiar roles.

This happens just the same way between human lovers. When one passes into the Higher Realm, he or she changes into a Being who can assist Earthly loved ones. But they do this from their advanced position, not the limited embodiment which the grieving ones long to see again.

It's all going to come out well in the long run. That quality of patience, which you're advising other pet owners to employ, is the exact and perfect quality that this whole experience is helping you to perfect in your own life –but on a larger scale!"

A COCKER SPANIEL'S DEATH AND HIS OWNER'S VISION OF HIM

Sarah writes: "Thank you, God, for finally bringing me to this blog! As You (God) know, I have been searching for others online who are interested in learning more about their pets– namely, the pet's specific role in a person's life– and I have been especially excited about sharing what happens to a beloved pet after it crosses to the other side. This prior sentence is a whole lot for someone who doesn't know me to swallow. That is, since you don't know me from anyone else you've encountered on the Internet, I make a bold assertion to imply that I might know what happens when a pet crosses over. But, here is the thing: I really believe I do, and I want to share what I know.

First, about me: I'm a mother of two, the wife of a physician, a former corporate professional who worked in an executive position, and a lifelong pet owner and animal-rights advocate. That's the surface me. But the "me" inside, usually only shared with family members and a lifelong friend, is a different story. Ever since I was a child, I have possessed what is referred to as Second Sight. Also, for as long as I can remember, I've been able to see things, in my mind's eye, that happen on the "Other Side." Or rather, I get glimpses and flash impressions. I've also had extremely detailed, past-life recollections from the time I was four-years-old. I'm now forty. I saw what happened to my grandmother when she passed over –which was confirmed by my father – since I reported images and descriptions that he knew about, but I'd never had exposure to.

But the most poignant thing happened recently, and that seemed to open a spiritual floodgate. Since it opened, I welcome it daily. My grandmother's brother passed away in January. But, here's the thing: none of us in my immediate family found out until a week after his death.

However, the very instant he died, I was asleep and I observed his passing in my dream. My grandmother was one of his escorts to the other side, and I heard an audible conversation between them that confirmed she had visited us after her death. When I woke from that dream, I wrote it all down, not knowing my great-uncle had just died, and thinking there was a deeper psychic meaning that I'd find out about later. Well, yes, there was a deeper meaning…I had actually observed his passing over.

When I "see" these things, I don't see detailed images of landscapes but literally "feel" the extreme joy and love contained in the Other Side. Well, I shouldn't even call it joy and love, because what I feel is so much more than that, and these words are only the closest approximation. Okay, after that happened, and I could no longer find rational explanations for what I was seeing, I accepted that I actually was seeing the spiritual world. I welcomed it.

Now, I'll cut to the chase, since this is directly related to animals and their incarnations. In February, our beloved cocker spaniel, Sammy, deteriorated after a short illness. It all happened quickly with no warning, and our vet wanted to put him to sleep that night. I decided to take him home to spend one last night with my son, whom Sammy had "guarded" all his life as his guardian angel. The next morning, we took Sammy to the vet so he could leave peacefully. He was suffering greatly by that time and was in profound pain.

But, each time I looked in Sammy's eyes, they would say, *"I have been in pain a long time. I have been hiding it. The boy needs me. He needs me more than anything, and I have to stand guard at my post until the very end."* Though he had a lot of Valium in his system, he kept trying to rally – even through the pain and heavy sedation. Even at death's door. I laid my hands on Sammy while my husband sobbed, looked at our darling dog and said:

"Sammy, you know you were our 'first son,' and you have given us tremendous joy and tremendous love. I don't have words to thank you for all that you have given us unselfishly. We love you now and we will love you always. You are the best dog we have ever had. I don't have words or even acts to repay the debt that I owe to you for giving all the love you had to the boys when they were going through hard times.

Sammy, you are an angel! But now you are tired and in pain. I see fear in your eyes. I see that you are afraid to leave our sons. I see that you think you are letting us down. You are not letting us down. You are a good dog...a good boy...and we love you. Please don't be afraid. Take all the time you need, and I will sit here, hold you, and talk to you. But please let go of the guilt that's holding you here. You're not letting us down."

Even through those words, Sammy kept trying to rally. I kept comforting him and telling him how much I loved him. It came to me to grab my iPhone and to play a song called "10,000 Reasons" by Matt Redman, and to sing the words to Sammy and pet him. Also, I sang along...

> **"Bless the Lord O my soul, O my soul, Worship His holy name, Sing like never before, O my soul, I'll worship Your holy name.**
> **The sun comes up and It's a new day dawning– It's time to sing Your song again, whatever may pass and whatever lies before me.**
> **Let me be singing when the evening comes.**
> **Bless the Lord O my soul, O my soul, Worship His holy name, Sing like never before, O my soul, I'll worship Your holy name.**

*You're rich in love and You're slow to anger.
Your name is great and Your heart is kind; For
all Your goodness I will keep on singing,
10,000 reasons for my heart to find.
And on that day when my strength is failing, the
end draws near and my time has come, still my
soul will sing Your praise unending,
10,000 years and then forever more."*

Finally, Sammy relaxed. So, I petted him some more and I told him that he was going to drift into a peaceful sleep. Just at that very moment, he was surrounded by loving angels that filled the room. I told him that when he woke up, he'd be with God, and that loving people, including my deceased grandfather, would come and escort him and that he would never be alone. I reassured him that we'd meet again one day, but that most of all, the gift of love and unselfishness that he gave the boys was so far and above any call of duty that any dog should ever have to take.

I told him to relax and to go with the angels. When he was sleeping peacefully, the vet readied the medication that would send him along. I told Sammy that I'd need to physically leave the room for that, but that I would be in the next room communing with his spirit so that he could make an easier transition. I reassured Sammy that my husband, his daddy, would hold him but that in order for me to get into a deep meditation to support him, I could not witness what was going to happen to his body.

So, I went into the next room, stilled myself, and contacted his spirit immediately, flooding it with pure love and coaxing him to the light in my mind's eye. My husband came out almost immediately after that, since Sammy literally went instantly as soon as the meds were administered. As soon as his spirit left his body, I felt Sammy's hesitation and his presence. I strongly coaxed him toward the light and flooded him with pure love.

Then my husband and I got in the car and I drove us around while my husband literally cried like he has never cried before. For my husband, some kind of well of pent-up emotion was tapped into, and he was able to cry for once in his life. Prior to that, he had been the type who literally did not have the ability to cry. After a few minutes, I sensed that Sammy had gone over. And I said reflexively and out loud, "God, is he all right?"

At that very moment, the song "10,000 Reasons" came on the radio station that I had on in the car.

Then, I was immediately flooded with a real-time image of Sammy playing in this electric-green field of grass. The reason I say "electric" green is because the color I saw in my mind's eye was green, but unlike any green on Earth. The color itself was pulsating and moving with vibrant life – and the hue was so much deeper, bolder, and brighter than anything seen here.

Then, I took a closer look at Sammy. He was restored to a "perfect" version of himself and appeared the way he was when he was about two-years old. Only he looked much better, and completely perfect. He was leaping and bounding and chasing beautiful, little white butterflies that were all around. Not biting them, but literally "leaping for joy" in the air, over and over again, realizing he had been freed from pain and all material constraints.

So, there he was, a perfect version of Sammy, leaping through beautiful, vibrating electric green hills, chasing gorgeous white butterflies. Finally, and briefly, in the distance, I saw my grandfather smiling at Sammy and watching him leap through the air, and I was reassured. I said an audible "Thank You" to God, and kept driving.

My husband, who is agnostic, but who wants to believe, was still sobbing at my side. I told him about the vision I'd just seen, and through tears, my husband said, *"I hope you are right. I want to believe you are right."* I knew that I was right because what I saw was not the stuff of a daydream or wishful thinking. But, that wasn't the only sign that was to come that day. I drove my husband to our house so that he could pick up his car and then follow me to another house that we were preparing to move into. On the way to the new house, I followed closely behind my husband in my own car. At one point, he was about fifty-feet ahead of me on a country road. I said silently. *"Please God! Please send my husband a sign that Sammy is okay."*

That instant, I noticed my husband slam the brakes of his car and stop in the middle of the road. I figured he'd halted for a deer and drove closer to his car. Then, I saw why he was stopping. I caught a quick glimpse of a beautiful golden tail wagging and bobbing, and then, a Golden Retriever stood in the road, wagging at him, and acting playful. My husband started to get out of the car to coax it out of the road, but as he did, the dog joyfully ran into the woods and was gone in an instant.

I immediately called him on my cell phone. I said, *"Wow, where did that gorgeous dog come from?"* He said, *"I don't know. I was driving and it literally just appeared in the road out of nowhere. So I slammed on my brakes. It disappeared just as quickly as it appeared."* Of course, I said excitedly, *"Honey, I was asking God to send you a sign that Sammy is okay, just as that dog came out of nowhere!"* Sammy and the dog from the woods were the exact same color and had a similar temperament. My husband said, *"Wow, that is a coincidence!"* I could tell he wanted some time in his own head, so I got off the phone and met him at the house.

Fast forward to today…. Since that day, I've certainly had the knowledge that Sammy is still very much with us, but also very much in a Higher Realm. My oldest son, the one that Sammy guarded, has many times heard Sammy scratching at the door in the middle of the night. Normally, he gets frightened very, very easily; but he tells me that when he "hears" Sammy, it's a comfort to him, because he knows Sammy is okay. My own parents, who don't even believe in this stuff, have also experienced similar signs.

But, there's more. For a couple of years prior to this, we'd been looking for an older Cavalier Spaniel to adopt to keep Sammy company. We had chosen a Cavalier because, years before, one had wandered into our yard and took to our family as if she wanted to be with us. We kept her until we got hold of her owner later that evening. But, each time I'd looked for a Cavalier, none were available.

Well, my oldest son was grieving hard over Sammy's loss, so now I had an unshakable wish to find a Cavalier. We ran a search online and found a perfect Cavalier puppy. The owners were thrilled, because the puppy had been posted for two weeks and no one had called. I agreed to buy it, but when I called the next day, the owner told me not to come because they had suddenly been flooded with calls, which led to a bidding war. Someone had purchased the puppy very late the night before. He laughed, said I had brought him good luck and gave a feeble "Sorry."

Well, I was disappointed and told him that we had lost Sammy the day before and that we were a bit let down. But, I wasn't angry. Five minutes later he called back, saying that his wife wanted me to come to meet the father of the puppies. So my dad, my boys and I headed out. My dad stayed in the minivan with the kids while I knocked on the door of the house where the Cavalier lived. My dad's passenger door was open in case I needed anything.

The minute that the people opened the door, the big Cavalier ran out to our minivan and jumped up on my dad's lap. Then he stood there, and wagged his tail. The owner said, "Well, I guess that is settled. He has chosen his new family!" Before I bought him, I asked the standard questions to get a sense of the dog's needs. His name was Hero, and his owner admitted that the dog had lived in their backyard kennel, day and night, since they'd only been using him to breed puppies. The wife said that when she heard my first phone call, she realized she'd need to stop breeding these dogs and give them to loving homes.

So, that's how I acquired Hero, a beautiful Cavalier Spaniel. He was sold to me with a broken jaw. This was something I found out from the dog, not from the original owners. My vet wired his jaw closed, and now, it's as good as new. When I first got Hero, he was certainly acting like a dog that had been severely abused. When I realized this, I told him that I was going to redeem his life, no matter what it took. And with the vet's help, he has been redeemed.

But what's even more amazing is now that Hero knows he's safe and loved, and that he'll always sleep on our bed with us each night with his own blankets, his personality has emerged. Not only is he an incredibly loving and smart dog, it's almost like he, literally, has the soul of a black Cavalier that we had when I was growing up.

That dog's name was Smokey, and he lived until he was nineteen-years-old. He passed away in my dad's arms. When Hero's owners opened the door that day, he didn't even stop to look, but made a beeline for my car and planted himself on my dad's lap, where Smokey had died! Now that his personality is coming out, the correlation between Hero's traits and Smokey's is 100%. The two dogs have the same identical quirky habits, and even the same bark – right down to the pitch. It literally is like Smokey chose to come back to our family.

Though this is probably uncommon, it would make sense, because Smokey was there for my dad when he was going through a horrible battle for tenure at a university. Smokey was the only thing that kept my dad alive. Now my dad is having a similar hard time, years later, and a dog who appears to be an incarnation of Smokey appears!

And I wouldn't have listened to the inner voice that urged me to look for a Cavalier if Sammy hadn't suddenly passed on! I have a lot more to say about this, but it's late and I need some shuteye. If there are other pet lovers out there who are interested in what happens to their beloved pet after they pass over, I sincerely hope this long comment offers comfort. I literally felt compelled to write it, so there must be a reason! I pray that it finds everyone who is in need of it.

With Love, Sarah"

DO PETS REINCARNATE AND CHOOSE THEIR OWNERS?

Oh my Holy Spirit! You mentioned that some animals also reincarnate. Do they choose their circumstances? Particularly, do they choose the individuals who wind up as their owners?

"Oh My Linda Layli, Layli Linda! We do have a few pets who come into specific homes, and therefore, they would be choosing those individuals to share their life with. Mostly, though, they come in as a general population because many animals are generic individuals of their species. For instance, most animals who become pets are treated so much like humans that they slip into their mode as a family member just as easily as another member of their breed would do. The relationship is made originally each time a new pet comes into a family.

But, in the past, someone might be getting a second chance and a specific animal might be a part of that drama. We'd arrange a life scenario including the same people and pets for another go-around. This describes past reincarnation epochs and not the current new millennium's plan, as things have changed considerably since the turn of the century, the year 2000. All is being started over, clean and clear; so this would no longer apply on Earth.

In the Heavenly Realms, many can still choose to live with beloved animals. There's so much love and harmony going on in those Higher Dimensions that it becomes natural to seek each other out. If you have love in your heart and sincerely wonderful memories, those consciousnesses will be pulled towards you in these more fluid realms. You can count on being with so many friends and loved ones, over and over again.

Life is lovely when you love and you are populating your own immediate universe as you go along, learning more and more about the intricacies of love. This is truly what life is all about. Pets tap into a certain vein of completely pure love, of which humans are capable only with non-human members of different species. This sort of love can also be tapped into on a planetary level when a human develops a passion for something really vast and high above them: like the fragile ecology, the space around our planet, astronomy or distant space bodies.

The Pet Sphere takes humans into association with something that's technically lower on the scale than they are. Some people will delve into microscopic regions, but it's difficult to identify human qualities in these levels; so the animal region is the only one in which love can flow so directly between hearts with something that isn't human. This is a great experience to have gone through within a life, and pets are doing wonderful things and a great service for mankind by accepting people into their own family loyalties. That happens when an animal accepts a human personality into its inner circle. Magic occurs – and the movement within both hearts is obvious and inescapable, even if it happens between strangers. A person's love capacity is affected if they have felt that movement, even once, during a material life – because it resembles normal relationships in the Heavenly Realm between consciousnesses that resonate together. Love is very lovely, as I've said before. And you love your pets like nothing else if this magic has occurred between you."

You've said that animals aren't here to discover spirituality, because they already have that Upper Connection. It sounds as if one of their functions is to trigger human emotions that couldn't be experienced any other way. Marriage is a valuable human learning experience that is not available through any other means; as is a human reaction to infants, especially one's own.

Each of these common themes is valuable, and each one falls into a distinct emotional category all its own. There's a purity of love and of loyalty that becomes very identifiable once it has been experienced. Of these episodes, only the pet love experience is unchanging. Marriages evolve and can dissipate, as far as intensity goes. Even an unconditional love for an infant frequently becomes morphed and complicated as the child grows. That love often becomes conditional, as do feelings for spouses. But a loyal love for a pet deepens over time, through a lifelong association with them. Once forged, that love and loyalty remains unconditional. That's pretty doggone miraculous, isn't it?

"You are tapping into realities that should be obvious to everyone. These feelings are pretty much the same for all humans who extend themselves to include an animal into their own personal heart and life space. This reality is open to everybody, but isn't accessed by all. And that's okay with Me.

It is a hidden reality within this smorgasbord of love, spread for your human race. This is one of the blessings flowing from your universe's bounties. Whether you take advantage of it or not is often up to your personal circumstances, but sometimes in life, people enjoy tasting the wonders of this quality and experiencing their capacity for love. Do you feel a heart-movement, a little flutter, or a pull in the chest when you communicate with a beloved pet friend? There it is! The purity of Love!"

PETS CAN CHOOSE WHETHER TO REINCARNATE AGAIN

Here's another answer to a question generated by the above post, almost a year later: Marilyn's fourteen-year-old dog, Bungie, died in her arms. She can't stop crying over his loss and asks about pet reincarnation. She wonders how, and when, their little souls enter their new bodies. At conception? At birth? At awareness of self? She can't stop hoping that Bungie will come back, and she also has the pull in her heart to bring home another little Sheltie. Oh my Holy Spirit! What is Your answer to Marilyn's questions?

"Oh My God! This is a wonderful Bungie dog! He is right here. Basically, all of these pets can choose what they want to do next because they're not in this world to improve themselves. They are here for the sake of their humans, and it's so good for these people. It's also important for Earth's supply of the loving quality, necessary for baseline functions performed by Creation Itself to maintain everything on this planet. We depend upon these pet combinations to help in the survival of all creatures. They counterbalance angry feelings that some humans always generate. Bungie has done well during his long stay upon this Earth, and I don't know if he wants to go down again.

Linda Layli, you are becoming the point of connection between these pets and their former owners. Basically, you are the Dead Dog Whisperer!

There's a bit of confusion about pet reincarnation. To these animals, an Earth life isn't as rewarding as life is in the Higher Realm, where they go when their physical life ends. So, to come back down again for the sake of a bereaved owner is a very large sacrifice. It often means, at least some of the time, that they will survive the death of that owner. Then, they must take what they get in the way of loving care for the balance of that little existence, which they extended only out of sheer love. Ironically and suddenly, they're now in the same grieving position that their beloved owner was once in.

You have all heard variations of the story of the loyal German Shepherd, who keeps vigil over his master's grave, going on seven years now. This is not a very happy position to be in, and every pet is glad to escape that necessity when they are the ones to die first. So, that's the dilemma at the core of these pet-reincarnation issues.

It's one thing to hope that a person will see their darling animal sweetheart at their own death during the famous meeting of loved ones, which greets successfully returning humans after death. But it's quite another thing to pray and beg for the return of that very same particle of spirituality to repeat its diminution back down to Earth in furry form for another long lifetime, just to fulfill those owner's wishes. Many do return, out of love for their owner, but they're not doing it for themselves and they're hoping that all will be well in this world below while on the alternative tour of duty.

Animals are always exposed to the heavy vibrations in the world, which they have come to counterbalance. Too often, many of these are found within the homes of loving owners: smoking habits, loud television or other electronic sources, family tensions, benign neglect, injury, illness, anger, and just general negative vibrations which are prevalent all over this basic-level planet.

Most owners are clueless about what they ask of their very-beloved pets. Addictions are the worst offenders. Anything that changes the optimal, normal human equation, whether it's in a smell or a taste, such as tobacco produces, or whether it alters behavior, is keenly felt by any animal exposed to it. They know a great deal more than any human can suspect.

Many times, it isn't their owner, but someone close to that person, who offends. Frequently, the undesirable equation goes on for years. Even the presence of rowdy, naughty children can make life very, very hard for an animal. I say all this, not to discourage anyone from being so in love with their pets that life is intolerable without them, but to educate people as to what pet reincarnation really means. An animal returns to an ideal condition after a tour of duty in a battleground environment on Planet Earth. Just as some soldiers will re-enlist, if required to do so; some pets will return for the sake of love. But, it's usually done at great sacrifice.

Ask yourself what you would do if a human love of yours so grieved over your death that they wished you back into their life as a newborn infant. Imagine that you had earned a lovely place in Heaven and were now weighing that against their desperate wishes to see and hold you once again. Would you have the maturity to know that the grieving one would ultimately recover from the shock of separation and would grow from the experience of finding new individuals to love? Even if those new babies, puppies, lovers, were not the same consciousness as yours?

On Earth, separation is normal. It's a condition of individuation. In these Upper Realms, which Bungie now occupies, togetherness can be constant, just as it is now, technically, between the two of you. Perhaps he's teaching you to adapt while you learn to "let go" so that you can accept your new condition, rather than insisting that things always remain the same. We suggest that you switch your affections to a new little puppy and allow both dogs to fill your life from now on: One, from Up Here, and the other, from within your loving arms. Bungie wants to say something now:

"*I love you, Mommy, and I, carefully, always will. But, it's time for you to let go of me so that I can be free to watch over you from Above. You have not been angry for a long, long, long time and it's good to let go of sadness and just be happy, happy, happy! I want you to let go of me, and everything that's making you so sad. And then, and only then, go out and find another little sweetheart to hold in your hands and in your heart. This is the best thing to do with us little creatures from this higher plane of existence. We can't talk when we get down to Earth, so all we can do is speak with our barks and our eyes. But many personal and private things can't be expressed that way.*

Maybe you will become instrumental in spreading this word around, about the purpose of pets, in the first place? Humans are learning unconditional love from us, and every single animal coming into your range of experience can teach those lessons. The more you help all animals, the more you grow as a human being and the better off the planet will become! It sounds too simple to be true, but that's the way that hidden meanings are tucked away, deep down in ordinary life, here in this boot camp of a planet.

So, my darling, Marilyn, I give you my blessings to love another dog as much as you loved me and to learn something about the deeper significances behind every little thing occurring on this planet of ours. I'll see you Up Here, Darling, but I don't want to reincarnate again. So, this is a good way to let you know that. It's not you! It's the wonderful position that

I'm enjoying right now. I can't wait to see you again and to take you for a long walk, just like we used to do!"

HOW DO YOU LIVE WITH EUTHANIZING YOUR PET!

Patricia writes: "You know it's funny! When I ask questions like this, I get an answer and the majority of the time, I already knew it. But it feels as if I'm remembering it rather than knowing it. My son seems to be a little bit closer to the spiritual realm than I am. When I adopted my dogs it was truly not the best plan for both dogs! It was just one of those things where, one day, I woke up and it was the thing to do. I'm not an impulsive person at all; I deliberate decisions to the point where I make myself crazy. Therefore those moments are rare. And when I'm impulsive, it sort of feels as if someone else is living my life for me.

I have had a decidedly terrible life! There are many people in other countries who have it worse, surely; but for me it has been endless spiritual and emotional warfare. I have been left shattered in every capacity, and living in third-world poverty as an American citizen. As it turns out, I'm quite good at it, really. However, in the midst of all of this, I was raped and had a child. That made a giant mess of whatever it was that I had built for myself, and it wrought a hurricane for me, thereafter. Still, those faithful mutts stood by me. I always joked that the two of them must have been my lovers in a past life, as the relationship we had was not typical, even by a dog person's standard.

So it came to pass a few months ago that some terrible things happened and I put the dogs down. I sit back and go over and over the scenario in my head, with different outcomes. Different things I could have done. The reality is that at a certain point when this decision was about to be made, it seemed like the entire world was screaming at me to put them down. I think from a legal standpoint, with the trouble the two of them had been in, no one would have argued. In fact, the veterinarian warned me that I could lose everything that I didn't have, if either of them behaved that way again.

I tried to listen to everyone. All I could think of was what we had been through, and how none of this was the dogs' battle. It was, decidedly, not mine either! But I was stuck in it. Otherwise, I would have had to put them in a rather uncomfortable position for several weeks. Again, I thought to myself: "When they had given me such a good reason to let them go, why would I torture them with quarantine?"

It has shattered me and my son. It's destroyed nearly every relationship (well those relationships needed to go away, anyway)... that I had. But, I see the dogs everywhere, out of the corner of my eye. I hear them sigh in the bedroom at night, or feel the weight of them on the bed. I get these little messages, here and there, a flooding of memories....I have to say, it's taught me a great deal about the truth of the spiritual realm in connection to this realm. I miss them dearly, but I also recognize how difficult their lives were because of the level of difficulty in my life. That was not my intention. It just happened.

My son told me the other night that he had a secret he had not wanted to tell me – he always knew that the dogs would die, and then come back to us. That he knew it would be hard but it would be okay. He is four! He is four-years-old, and plays with Legos all day, and turns into a tiny Buddha, randomly!

I guess I feel horribly guilty that I put my dogs down. I'd almost been hit by a car several times in the days leading up to it. I was about to lose our home and my job, again, due to the individuals contributing to my dogs' trouble. The farm dog had been poisoned. I had my tires slashed. My car was dying. My child was out of control, and the people in my life were going out of their way to be unreasonably manipulative. It was like reliving the same circumstance that had put me in this bad position in the first place!

I sit here and think to myself, that I do have PTSD. And, essentially, my dogs died because I couldn't wade my way out of trying to decide between what was a real threat and what was not. All I knew was that I would not tolerate anything else happening to them because of me, or my decisions, or my inability to get out of this mess. One dog was nearly twelve. He had arthritis, bilateral knee surgeries, senility and a little blindness. I feel less bad about his death, as dogs like that typically go downhill quickly, and I'd rather have him go in peace while he was happy and still able to get around.

The other one was just middle-aged, happy and healthy. If you never saw him take down a deer or some livestock all by himself, you'd think he was a companion animal. But that habit, in the end, wound up costing him his life! Seven goats, in under ten minutes! That's how long it took me to brave an electric fence and tackle him, as he chomped on a goat's face. He took out the top seven milkers on our farm, out of a herd of fifty. He ran around the herd, looking for just the right goats; injuring the best milker and the worst. Other goats' injuries were less serious. Oliver, my older dog, bit a man soon after. The guy deserved it by kicking him. But in these cases, it's always the dog's fault. Oliver had been fear-biting all his life. He bit someone a year ago, as well, but that individual didn't press charges.

Anyway, I'm babbling on because I'm so heartbroken. I wanted them to have a good home. But the one was literally suicidal without me, and the other? Well, it took three years to make him my dog and I don't know many people who could put up with what that dog had to dish out!

I loved them endlessly. I guess, I wish I could communicate clearly; as in, not the mixed messages and images and the thinking that they are outside, if I would just open the door. And they are not! If I were these two dogs, I'd probably not reincarnate. But, I would hope... you know, one day, when things are better for my son and me....I'm terrified to be without dog-protection!

I hated that in the end, their bad habits reflected, so distinctly, what they had survived with me. I've been alone most of my life... but I wasn't alone when I was with them. When I look back on the tragedy, I don't really see it. I see them, and how, if I hadn't endured all of that, I would have never known them or the love that they had. I'm only here today because of them... in so many ways. Thoughts?

Because I'm traveling in Uruguay, I haven't had much computer time. So, until I could take dictation, I've corresponded with Patricia, (now, Trish), especially to encourage her to continue writing her experiences, as something struck me that she may have an unusual story to tell. Indeed, she does! Perhaps, we can share that too. Oh My Holy Spirit! Can You help Trish to deal with the euthanasia that she was forced to do for both of her beloved dogs?

"Oh My Linda Layli! You told her the truth... that death doesn't hurt anybody, ever! And that is just that! She's doing much better now. This was the purpose of the life of those wonderful dogs that she had to put down because they attacked and killed so many goats in the milking herd.

There's a dichotomy in that story, which you discerned while thinking about it. Yes, the goats of that herd weren't being executed by the dairy farmer, because they were necessary to his business...at that time! But, you can be sure that those same goats would not live on, benevolently, forever. Most farm animals get slaughtered by their own farmer, himself, for table meat. So, it's only a big show... and all, economically-based, with the official outrage against the dogs for doing, so rapidly and wastefully, what the goat farmer had in mind for them all along.

The only difference to the human mind was that the farmer had the moral right to slaughter the goats, and the dogs did not! Tell Patricia that her dogs didn't mind going out in a blaze of glory, and now they can stay, indefinitely, around their little family and help her fortunes to improve.

It's The Power of Story that Trish has to do something about and that's why you're encouraging her to write her tale. She must get it out of herself in order to face the future with this precious child, who has been through such traditional fires with her. Many are of her own making, but some are through a strange society's practices.

Victimization of a woman, when she gives away her personal power to a man in the role of husband, has been going on for far too long. The Voiceless will find their voice in this new millennium and accounts of these crimes against a woman will help to free them, collectively, in the future. Her motive should not be to get Justice; but, simply to open the book on the subject and join other brave women with a story to tell. It may be her only way to tell her son about his roots and remembered terrors. This writing has nothing to do with making her rich, which most books don't do, anyway. Nor to get justice for the guilty.

It's just that she does have a talent to express these things, and she is being encouraged from The Other Side – by her two Guardian Angel dogs – to get started rebuilding herself, emotionally. This can begin with a clear analysis of the circumstances. She must leave off the victimization role. It doesn't serve her, at all. These beautiful, beautiful dogs are expressing their heartfelt wishes that she and the boy will find some peace and happiness wherever they are in this life. For these pets, that death was merciful, and they thank her for it!"

THE DEATH OF YOUR PET TEACHES YOU DETACHMENT

Ela Singh writes: "My lovely dog, Leechi, died in my arms. Her death has completely devastated me. We were soul mates. I have still not gotten over her death and don't think I ever will. My question is: "Will she come back to me in my life?" Please answer. Thank you."

Oh my Holy Spirit! What can You say to comfort Ela?

"Well, I cannot promise anything about your dear doggie, Leechi, returning in this particular life. The important thing is to go ahead with your own life intact and take to heart the things that Leechi brought to you in the first place! A dog is just an innocent partner in a human's life. Independence is the key to spirituality, and that shapes and determines the strength of the human soul. Too much dependence upon other people, or your pets, hampers the progress of your own soul. So does overwhelming grief, because you cannot see clearly ahead when you are mourning so heavily that you wish only for the past to continue.

No! Leechi is not coming back to you, but she will be waiting at the Gate when you come through it. You must cheer up and carry on your life without her! It's not impossible, you know, and there are strengths within you that she is now causing you to discover.

People! Don't do this to your pets, or to your human loved ones, when they pass on! Let them go! You would not like it if someone living clings to you, psychically, mentally and spiritually; once you pass over into the wider world beyond life. Just let them have their freedom while you soldier on with your Earth life. It will all get sorted out in time. This could well be your own Lesson in Detachment!"

EVEN THE DEATH OF A TINY PET LEAVES BIG HOLES

Claudine writes: "My precious little ferret, Cocotte, crossed over a week ago. I can still feel her in our house, sleeping in her "mother's" (my sister's) bedroom. She went downhill so fast her little body could not take more; we had to make the impossible decision to let her go. I just want to know…. Is she ok?! Is she still beautiful as she used to be?... And most of all... I want her to know that she changed our lives, and that we will love her forever and ever. I miss you toutouneskiski!

Hello Madame J. Brown, (Sorry in advance for my English, it's not my first language) Even if it took some time for you to answer us, don't worry the timing was perfect for me. Your email came in a dark hour to put some light back when I was doubting life and its purpose...

Losing my beloved pet ferret, Cocotte, is probably the hardest pain I have ever encountered. Many members of my family have crossed over – yes it is painful and the grief is long – but this is different. As you said in your reading, and you really put your finger on it, it actually feels like losing a precious child, but with more fur.

I still have lots and lots and questions about my precious little cat-snake, and the answers you gave us added more questions! I kind of always knew they weren't from this planet. They are innocence, purity and love, wrapped in long, fluffy bodies! Thank you for taking the time to answer our questions. It's like another push forward, because in moments like this, I swear time is probably really stopping. Thank you. Thank you.

Ah, and one quick question: do you have any books you would recommend that I need to read? Thank you, Claudine."

Hi Claudine, it's Linda, finally able to answer your letter.

My goodness, it was wonderful to hear from you. And never apologize for your English... it's perfectly beautiful! I'll bet that what you are really experiencing is GRIEF! Just plain old, deep-down, gut-wrenching grief, and that is actually a great measure of the LOVE that you had for your little darling! You still have, and always will have, that huge quality and quantity of love for your sweet little furball. And to be honest, you'd never want the love to go away.

And just because the quality of this feeling is worse than the grief you also feel about your departed family members, it doesn't mean that isn't grief, too. Can you admit that you were in-love with your pet? But not "in-love" with the ones of the family? It just hurts so much not to have the object of that extreme love with you anymore. Maybe it would help, though, to get another sweet creature to feel that same kind of love for?

I'll bet that you would not be so truly worried about what's happening in Heaven, if you really stopped to analyze this. After all, why would God's little innocent beings have anything to suffer about? Life is shorter for animals than it is for humans, so the potential for Cocotte to die early was pretty high, even if her life wasn't as long as you expected. The Upper Plane, where we all wind up, sooner or later, is a higher evolution than Earth is. Planet Earth is hard; the Home Place is not! It is saturated with happiness.

So, sit down, take a deep breath – and think about this, carefully and honestly. Can you possibly shift all that pain to the idea that it is grief, and not fear of your baby's welfare, that has you tied in such knots? Grief is normal, and it's located right inside of your body and your mind. It may take some time to disappear, but it will start to dull and then recede, because that's normal, too. The love doesn't go but the separation agony will ease off. We humans couldn't stand it if it didn't.

But, guess what? That agony shields you from any feelings that your departed sweetie pie might send your way. The departed pets have to wait until their survivor calms down. I can't make any promises that you'll ever feel anything from the Other Side because it's not automatic – and in fact, actually quite rare. But, consider that Cocotte is probably able to tune into your emotions all the time. Right now, your sadness isn't what she's used to feeling from you.

Maybe this whole experience is designed to help you grapple with your beliefs? Maybe you doubt that there can be anyplace better than Earth? So, this little fur-covered child has a huge lesson to deliver, if you'll only stop banging your head against that wall. Can an animal teach a spiritual lesson? Give her a little help and open your mind and heart to all these exciting truths that have recently been flooding down to us.

First, go to YouTube and just romp around in all the Life After Death material you can find. There are many recorded talks of all sorts. Since animals populate those Upper Regions too, you can be sure that what you read about humans, as far as their welcome atmosphere and surroundings, will be true for animals...except that they aren't under so many tests and challenges to improve themselves. They already ARE. But, the idea is that it's a pretty cushy place, all right, and you'll be there too someday. And that little sweetie pie will be at the front of the line to greet you. Everything about the Upper Kingdoms is positive.

Then, Google "Eben Alexander, MD, author of 'Heaven Is Real'" and just digest anything he says. He's a neurosurgeon, who clinically died of meningitis and then came back from a seven-day coma. He had a near-death experience (NDE) and now is a full-time lecturer and author about it. It was that wonderful! He still practices medicine, but is fully devoted to sharing his experience in "the Gateway and the Core" that he found during his time on the Other Side. He was pretty much an atheist scientist before he met God and learned the truth by dying. Read anything by Brian Weiss, MD, or Michael Newton, PhD, or Robert Schwartz. In fact, find NDE stories. They all describe the same thing.

Or start tackling this from the standpoint of grief. See if there are some support groups you can go to. I don't think this is worry. I think it's grief, and it's probably Training Day designed by your Darling. Try to see the humor in that! And she won't be jealous if you bring another little sweetie pie home with you to be an Earth-based teacher for you. Someday, you'll see how much FUN this subject can be. You'll be fine!

Oh my Holy Spirit! Rather than asking a specific question, do You have any message or thoughts for Claudine?

"Y.E.S! I sure do! My God! We are so glad that you are going to open this subject! We want to tell you something and you must listen to Us very, very carefully, Linda Layli. We don't want you to become a personal psychic either, but you must counsel these people who write in to you asking for help with their dearly-departed pets, because they have to learn what it is that their pets are trying to teach them. And you have been selected to try and get things across! So, I don't care if you decide to do personal, psychic readings for animals. Just don't go into the realm of dead people! Leave that to the regular psychics!"

Oh, my goodness! The Dead Pet Whisperer? I was just joking about that title a while ago! I don't have much confidence about my abilities, but I never have had, in any of these new fields that You have pushed me into. Have I?

"Oh My God! No! No, you have not! It's just that animals have a Voice too, and they have very few psychics to speak through. And now, they can talk to you, so let's just go ahead and see what happens. Do you want to talk to Cocotte? Here she is!"

"Okay, Linda Layli, Layli Linda! I want you to know that I am really, really pleased that you are willing to do this. Speaking for all animals, we are so glad to get someone who will talk to us, instead of just patting us on the head and going about their business without wondering what we have to tell them. I'm so happy to be able to report that my own Mama, Claudine, is very good at communicating with us herself, and I hope that she will get into that routine again. Even a little bit, not much! I don't want to make her turn away from the world and start living in this Realm Above before she is scheduled to come Up Here.

Listen to me, Linda Layli, Layli Linda… or Linda J. Brown, my good new friend. We animals have to keep safe and sorry, all at the same time. We don't think that you will understand this, because you are not an animal. So, I will explain:

Our job on Earth is twofold. It is one of the most delicate jobs we have ever done, for it is dangerous for anybody to fall as far in love as Claudine has. She turned her heart inside-out for me. I did not criticize her at the time because I could not get away from my own feelings for her. Basically, we did not have to explain anything to each other. Our pure hearts got really bonded together.

Part of our job – Listen to me! – is to bring Love to the planet. That's what all animals do, though many

have nothing to do with humanity and we spread Love mostly among each other. But, now and then, we feel so sorry for humans because we know we will die someday and it's going to be a lot sooner than our humans will die and we're going to leave them alone, unguarded, in this tough place of the Earth World. We can only hope that we have loved them sufficiently to protect them from harm when we go back to our Home, where we will refill our own storage batteries.

Oh my God! Claudine loves me! There's so much to know about Love, though, and one thing that Earthlings do know about Love... it sounds horrible, but it's true, true, true. That Love can hurt people so much when it goes away from them. Energies can't travel very far, from Up to Down, if they have pain in their hearts caused by pure Love. So, that's why we have really had so much trouble in setting things up, Down Here on Earth. Basically, we want this Love to connect the two Planes."

Maybe you, Cocotte, are the needle and Love is the thread; but pain and sorrow make the fabric so tough, that you can't finish your work in drawing these places, and all the hearts in both Kingdoms, closer together?

"That is so poetic, Linda Layli, because that just says it in a nutshell!"

Ohhhhh, here's another strange twist between these conditions: When on Earth, animals are originally designed to live out of doors, taking their chances with the weather, the food supply and the predators. Then, some of you become pets, doted upon by your loving owners, who would worry just as much as Claudine worries now, if you ever get lost and return to the wild. But, when an animal finally returns to its Home In Heaven (I hear that it's Fantastic!), and you leave this rough-edged survival existence here in the boot camp of Earth... Wellllll, these same loving owners become frantic about your survival skills!

Or else, the people without belief of continuation after death (which isn't true of your Mama!) can't stand the thought of their helpless baby facing oblivion! Are you trying to tell us that Earth is the oblivion and you are all here to bring us Home by using your strong ability to Love us as you do?

"My God, Linda Layli! This is The Holy Spirit! Yes, yes, yes! That is the whole thing in a nutshell! You cannot tell Me that you are not My Dead Pet Whisperer!"

Excuse me! This is your little, worshiping Cocotte! This is my interview! Let me finish here! Okay, Linda Layli, tell my Mama Claudine that she has now served her purpose concerning my death. It had to happen this way so that she would write to you and you would have to talk to me and then begin doing your job as The Dead Pet Whisperer! That's all there is to it! Sincerely, all there is to it!

All right, Linda Layli, now you can send this to Claudine and we will continue to be safe... but not sorry, anymore. As she clears her anxiety field, I will continue to come to her and we'll have our old chats just like we did when I was alive. It's not the end of the world, you know! Someday, I will come and get her and bring her up to these beautiful, paradisiacal fields.

I have to go now! It's dinnertime here and the Mama whom I had abandoned to go down to Earth is waiting for me to come to my bowl.

Life goes on everywhere, Sweetheart! Or don't you know that?"

CLAUDINE'S REPLY TO THE MESSAGE FROM HER DEAD PET FERRET, COCOTTE

"Good morning Linda Layli, Wow... just wow.... The conversation yesterday was a real breakthrough for all of us...

and I'm not going to hide from you the fact that I was deeply moved by all this and burst into tears....

It was hard to go to sleep after that, as my mind was running wild.... But I had a dream where Cocotte was with me. She was whole and beautiful as always, but very weak. I had to put her in my pocket (?!) to take her home, and then I realized she was pregnant and she gave birth to three or five baby ferrets.... I started to place them in a warm blanket when we reached our destination... aaannnd my alarm took me back to the physical world for another day. When I woke up, I felt like I had to tell you this. Not sure why, but there it is!

It's a real blessing that I have found you when I was wandering around the Internet for answers. Sincerely, I think I have looked at and read pretty much all the available sources on the subject, but you are the one and only one where I left a message.

You know when she did her little "appearance of smoothness"*(apparition de douceur* as I used to say it), and poked her beautiful nose at me:), that she never liked to be disturbed when she was doing her things. Like sleeping! Ahaha! So I'm pretty sure it's the same in the *Other Life* and she will still do as she pleases. But if she thinks of things she wants to share with us, my heart is open to her as always.

I don't know why she didn't mention her other mother, Vanessa, my sister, but my feeling is it's probably because Vanessa is so closed to anything right now, and her beliefs are still those of a very doubting person. I love my sister with all my soul, and Cocotte was like the heart and the living fluffy bond between us. Maybe that's one of the reasons why I felt so close to Cocotte, and always loved to give her nice and white protective energy.

I still do that with my other two ferret babies, Plushie and Kettens. Cocotte appeared in our lives when we were in deep depression, both of us. We didn't want pets because we knew how heartbreaking it is when they go; but we took her home and our story of changing and informing the world for them started.

So many things to say… but I have to go to work! Thank you so much… thank you thank you. Sending lots of love and good vibes to you. Thank you. Claudine"

HOW WOULD I KNOW IF MY DEAD GRAM, OR MY DEPARTED DOG, IS NEAR ME?

Savana wrote to ask:"How would I know if my dead gram is near me?"

I know that, in this chapter, we're speaking of animals and pets, but these answers prove that there's very little difference in some relationships between the living and those who have passed over to their next world's condition. Oh, my Holy Spirit! Savana has asked this sweet, simple, but very deeply emotional question. What would You like to say to her?

"The answer is always the same thing. It is always the same cosmic answer *(That they are happy!)* for every person and animal who arrives in the Upper Realms. But Savana has posed her question in a general way, asking how she would feel or how she can tell if her dead grandmother is with her? So, let's answer her in a general way because many people wonder the same thing. However, one answer might not apply to all of them.

That's what We are aiming at: to help as many people as We can – because there's a great deal of individual expression possible between these two planes of existence. If someone doesn't find their particular experience or sensation listed in someone else's answer; then they might discount their own, very different, impressions. And We might have done some harm since Our answers can't possibly cover all of the ways that a soul might choose to get in touch with a living being. Everything might be useful to break through in this type of delicate opening between beloved souls."

Oh, my Holy Spirit! In this one answer of Yours, so far, You appear to be contradicting Yourself. But, I think I know what You mean:

1. That "the answer is always the same" means that when death occurs, the person's or pet's soul always survives and is very close to its beloved ones, especially when that living person is thinking about and praying for them, missing them, and wondering if they are still all right. That reality is 100% in effect with every death. Bonded hearts remain bonded and the departed one is dependably aware and nearby, except that the living can't usually pick up the clues unless their own Inner Channels are fully functioning. Even then, we humans tend to doubt our dreams and impressions, and we seek confirmation from others who offer psychic services.

But, in this first instance, which is really about whether that Loved One actually "survived" death and is happy... or even okay... the answer is dependably the same for everyone. Is that correct, oh my Love?

"Every human who dies is in this same happy position, even if Earth does not approve of some of their behavior. Everyone receives counseling Up Here, and plenty of help and encouragement for their own future development. But they're all much better off when they arrive in this Heavenly Home, where they originated before their courageous leap into an Earth life. So, yes, that is 100% the happy answer for all who have come through death."

2. But, Savana's question was more long-term – and it sounds as if she suspects her grandmother's continued presence in her life. She probably feels sensations or finds clues, but she would like to verify that, instead of thinking she's crazy or making things up. So, Your second statement suggests that there could be a great variety of ways that a soul can connect with the living, and that one list might not satisfy them all. Is this also correct?

"Absolutely! Many attempts are usually made before giving up! And this doesn't always happen between the living and the dead. It's very, very, very individual!

Savana, just Trust The Process! If you suspect her presence, then it's probably true! You can continue to be yourself, just as you always were with her. She is also the same... so, you be just the same! Talk to her any way you want to – and I would suggest digging into the literature on this subject – because many things will resonate in your heart, and these will be the ones that apply to your situation. Your grandmother can help you grow in understanding, as she always has!

Thank you for asking this question, because it's vital for humans to overcome their fear of death and their worry about the Other Side. If you only knew! Usually, that's what your departed one is trying to tell you. In every case, they are happier now than they were in the Earthly plane of existence. So, that's their glad tidings!

Ever since you and I started talking and laughing together, Linda Layli, Layli Linda, I've wanted to bring you Up Here and show you around this Kingdom. But, it's not time for you yet, so you'll have to wait quite awhile. If everyone knew what it's like after one dies, there would be no mourning at all. Just a beautiful realization, as if they had gone to the most spectacular garden of all, in some classic vacation spot that everyone wants to visit in their fondest dreams. So, that's usually the message they have for their survivors.

Suffering goes away, and they remember what they had to forget before they came down to an Earth life. They are now Home, surrounded by old friends. That's usually the contents of their "Earmail" that they try to send back to their dear ones on Earth."

Jennifer writes:

Hello, my name is Jennifer. I would like to know something. I think that it is too obvious that I have lost a friend. My Siberian Husky, Mikka, passed away yesterday. Today my husband and I went and got memory tattoos for our loss. She was very loved, and we don't know what happened to her, for her to die. We came home from work and found her body. I thought that she could have gotten into something, but that's not the case. I thought that she could have been attacked, but that was not the case either. My husband thinks that she had a heart attack after getting too excited. I feel so horrible at the moment. She did not live a long life. She was almost two-years-old.

But fast forward to getting the tattoos. At the tattoo shop, I was looking around and saw a toy car on the floor with Mikka's name on it. Does anyone think this is her way of showing me that she'll be coming back to me soon? I also have another Siberian husky, who's about a month pregnant right now. Does anyone think that it could be an upcoming pup? I would like some feedback on this to give me that little glimmer of hope. Thank you.

Katja writes:

I must say I never considered this…about dogs being left behind for years after their human passed…when I was feeling desperation for my elderly dog to stay with me. What if she chooses to come back after she dies, wanting desperately to stay with me? I have a younger dog and I never considered, when I bought him a few years back, that he might be her "next body" so she could stay. She hated him at first; then suddenly, they became friends! What if it's because their spirits have already communicated and she knows he is going to "step aside" when her current body fails, so that she could occupy it?

How would I know if she has transitioned into his body? Or whether he wanted to stay and likes having me as his mum? I rescued him from a puppy farm, from having nothing… to lots of toys, being loved and having a "big sister," my older dog.

What if she decided to go to the Rainbow Bridge for a while to rest and then come back as an older rescue, so she could spend our (mine and my younger dog's) remaining time with us but not be left behind here herself for years? How would I know this was what she was planning to do?

Katya, you're worrying too much about something that's impossible to understand – and reincarnation has never been usual in the animal kingdom. Dogs know nothing about such things before their death, as is true of humans. Could you plan your next life before this one is over? Besides, reincarnation has been discontinued in this new millennium, so just enjoy both pets during the time you have left with them. You'll all meet again when the time is right.

Oh my Holy Spirit, so many people worry about their beloved pets and feel so sorry for them in the sudden separation that death brings. On Earth, the pet was dependent upon the human owner for its very life and welfare... just like a small child is lost without its parents. When an animal is ripped from them, the owners grieve for their loss, but also worry immensely about how that dear little soul can continue alone. What is Your Advice to these wonderful humans? We have so little information about an animal's survival of death.

"Not every animal survives death, as their souls and their spiritual histories and trajectories are in another category from those of humans. Sometimes these creatures, these beautiful creatures, are not at all from this planet and they don't experience anything like death. They simply transition to another place, without going through the human soul's program. So, it's impossible to compare the two.

But, Love is Love, and that is a bonding that will continue in Heaven and on Earth. So, that's why you will find your pets waiting for you in the Next World, and sometimes, in other future lives. You can also feel them around you if they have passed on. Many books exist about these subjects. Everyone can learn a great deal from those sincere and guided authors. I highly recommend them!"

DO HUMANS REINCARNATE AS ANIMALS? PETS AS HUMANS?

Today, I had a great conversation in the hostel, with a mother, Miquelina, and her daughter Carla, who are here in Montevideo, Uruguay, to see the Paul McCartney concert tonight. Miquelina had a question for The Holy Spirit, as to whether she had lived many former lives and whether some of them might have been as an animal? I explained that I didn't deal with personal psychic questions, but that the animal-to-human question had never been dealt with on my blog, so let's ask.

Oh, my Holy Spirit! Do any humans ever reincarnate as animals or do any animals get reborn as humans?

"Oh, My Linda Layli! No! No! No! Practically never! It used to be done, sparingly, to punish a human, if they had behaved like an animal in their lifetime, taking what they wanted in cruel, cruel ways. Though exactly that same behavior might be expected of a fierce animal in the course of its daily life, living a normal animal existence, it is not expected of the higher, human species. So, no, it's not practical to do anything like a movement between species…even within the animal kingdom.

But, there are humans who have special affinities for certain animals, or for animals in general, and they're actually expected to work closely with those whom they feel akin to. They will connect on a spiritually deep level, which helps both the humans and those animals to understand each other better."

CHAPTER TWO
THE NEW MILLENNIUM AND VOICE HEARING

HEARING YOUR INNER VOICE AND ANSWERING IT

Time went through a revolution of gears on New Year's Day, 2000, and we all moved. Not only to a new century – but to a new Millennium! That's an undeniable fact, well-deserving of our attention, whether we have any personal drama attached to it or not. Many Christians still await The Rapture in a diverse set of forms, depending upon the branch of Christianity. But surely, other cultures must put stock in this time shift as well. Who? Why? I can't believe that we were all so blasé.

Apocalyptic measures do seem to be waiting in the wings these days. Quietly. Unbeknownst to the public, software experts now work overtime to avert a global, digital collapse, sure to strike, according to them, on January 19, 2038, unless geniuses can squirrel out extensive, split-second-counting roots. Leftover from Y2K is a most insidious bug built into all UNIX systems, called **"The 2038 Bug."** This so-called threat originated with wrap-around dates in the 1970s because those early program writers never expected their comparatively-amateurish designs to still be our basic digital foundation, fifty years later. If we can't conquer the **2038 Bug,** some say that Earth may experience that prophesied lights-out period, after all. Doesn't this sound familiar?

In addition, our present worldwide proliferation of nuclear weapons could, accidentally, trigger World War Three: a globe-engulfing holocaust to make Nagasaki and Hiroshima pale by comparison. Not only would such a calamity fulfill ancient prophecy, but, according to some surprisingly original statements contained herein, it would cause the "long-fearedby-the-Sci-Fi-community's" deadly execution of Earth by an unrealized, overseeing space authority– and The Intergalactic Federation would step in to protect other planets from Earth's aggressiveness!!!???

However, for Earthlings in 2015, these anciently-foretold events certainly don't cause us to lose any sleep. Either we've never heard of such, or we simply don't believe in them. Frankly, there's nothing that we, as individuals, can do about speculations of lurking, negative possibilities. Collectively, we could stay the hand of aggressors who would bring us to the brink of war, and I do believe that we're already devoted to that end. We all want peace. Not only in our hearts, but in our lands. Grand and global statements aside, this book is not a treatise containing such massive proportions as a global, millennial end times.

It's merely a collection of questions from the public. A large basket of delicate eggs, which I'm now shoe-horning into the boot of a single book in order to demonstrate that it is possible to live a life on Earth while maintaining an active association with Those in an Upper Dimension. We can speak to our departed loved ones. Even if they are animals. We can sometimes hear words within our heads. When any question is asked, understanding follows. Eggs are always broken to feed us. Perhaps I'm a chef, serving up a tasty omelet? Or inventing a cake mix, over which I shall pour chocolate sauce to make it even more delectable; in order to suggest that you might try it for yourself.

Here's my rationale: Within these answering words, dropped from Above, I've detected one common theme of hope, showing up now and then as a golden thread, to tie these random subjects together.

That recurring theme is found in an Upper admission that the present millennial rollover marks the end of a long testing period for humans, during which we were studied as to our individual choices between positive and negative behavior. Free Will to choose for ourselves was stringently protected by a

Heavenly hands-off policy. Even memories of our past lives were diligently erased for each new human reincarnation.

At the end of this testing period, grades were given; conclusions drawn; experiments ended; laboratories on the matter made obsolete. Earth was, in fact, let out of school. All such scientific studies, eventually, do come to their foreordained end. This was the true significance of Y2K, our foretold End Time!

Within the Test, during past millennia, God judiciously called to us through His Chosen Ones; who came to this planet specifically to remind us of His Presence and to teach us how to connect with Him through prayer. Of course, They each left a large body of scriptural information, guidance and examples, which now permeate our present-day cultures and are the basis of everyone's spiritual life. However, their similarities have been overlooked, in favor of the inevitable, external differences. Many wars have been fought by sincere believers on each side, who think that they are each other's enemies.

All the while, The Holy Spirit provided God's direct line to every individual. He has always been our own individual "telephone line" to God, Whom I address as The Great Creative Force.

"The Holy Spirit wants your call. He will patch you through, immediately, to speak to your Creator!"

That enemy-issue between humans could have been cleared up, in no time flat! But, generally, the idea that after prayer, "we'd hear a Voice in return" was never mentioned in the scriptures. Oh, we might receive *results*, of course, but not God's Own Self talking to us, said the clergy. All claims of such were frowned upon and made suspicious by almost every religion.

To this day, any claimant to have God on the other end of the line risks a special suite in the Schizoid Hotel. Believe me, I know whereof I speak! And I'm truly grateful now for that kneejerk reaction from the medical community. I'm actually so pleased to be able to put pay to their assumptions on behalf of all of us Voice-Hearers! Little did those doctors suspect that thirty-five years later, I'd call on everyone to listen carefully for that small, still, Voice within their inner ear!

That's why the common thread claimed by this book is still radical enough to raise eyebrows... and suspicions. Sometimes, even voices from the throats of men! A personal conversation with The Holy Spirit? Nonsense! Not only does this common theme claim:

"When you call, He will answer!" It goes a giant step further, to assure that, now:

"He will call, and you can listen, and then answer!
Then, He will listen to you, and answer your own words!"

And why not? The long test is over! God can initiate His love affair with His creatures, once again, because He now has the results on His two scientifically-creational questions:

1. "How would 'I,' as a human being, behave in any given situation?"

2. "Would I, could I, as mankind, turn around and recognize Myself through the murk of materiality?"

Finally, with a mixed bag of results, there's no longer any reason for a hands-off game plan. Maybe you will hear directly, from Him, as I first did in 1980? For goodness' sake, don't waste the next fifteen years trying to deny that you heard any Voice except your own ego, as I did! Thank goodness, He gave me a second chance in 1995 to realize that such a startling invitation wasn't simply my own wishful thinking!

As of this new millennium, God will be whispering into your ear His loving invitation to join Him in the dance! Please, my darling people! Please, listen for His sweet call, spoken to you directly inside of your head, directly to your inner ear. It is genuine! It is real! It is from the positive realm! From The Heavenly Kingdom!

It has come to open your inner hearing channels, so that you may now not only hear The Voice of God, but that you may answer in return and be heard by Him. Now, you may have a genuine, two-way conversation. The long test is over! You need not simply say your prayers and walk away. Now, you're being invited to listen to His Answer and to live your life in full communion: God's Mind to your mind! Your mind to His Mind!

This is the funny thing that happened, oh so quietly, and oh so naturally, on the way to the Year 2000... the Millennial Rollover... which no one paid much attention to. The barriers came down between God and Man! This is a brand-new day, and it's a clean slate for us all. Nothing is the same as yesterday, and we have nothing to prove to God that He hasn't already figured out about us!

So, the work right now is to find a way to talk to Him about it. Of course, we will do that at death. But, to do so during life...ahhhhh, what a rare treat that might be!

Those who "catch the vision," who "hear the Voice or the music, or see the lights" are privileged, as always, to spread the love. Right at first, though, love of God is not a collective act; at least, not until each heart goes within and stays with Him, personally and alone. Then, we can all enjoy the group effect. We can help each other but we can't meddle. Only The Holy Spirit needs to intervene between each one of us and our Creator.

Oh, it's fine, if we drop a hint to others of how to do this. Softly, helpfully. Each in our own way. At best, we might simply be spraying a little oil into a rusty heart lock; or introducing our own Inner Lover to someone who longs for Him, but can't see how to make the move from "Here" to "There." Humans will always have Free Will, but sometimes, they're shy or bruised with disappointment. They don't know how to walk across the floor and ask for that first dance with God. There was a time when the human had to supplicate in prayer first to enable Him to interfere with our free will. With the new millennium, the rules have changed. The test is over and God will come a-courting.

Oh my Holy Spirit, why do we appoint millennial qualities to a date on a particular Earth's calendar, dating from the birth of Christ? There are many other calendars, some based on the lives of other Revelators, though not universally in use today. Is that the answer? That this calendar is used universally?

"Yes, that's all that it is. We started each of these calendars, even the Mayan one. It's not only necessary to mark the dates on every planet, but it's part of the overall sphere of Time. This is one of the great mysteries of the universe; that time is coordinated throughout the universal domains and each place of existence behaves as a cog in a gigantic clock. We reset the time on every planet according to a timetable that's so very vast that it's not detectable to any of the creatures."

By now, we know that Earth is a small, circulating particle in a moving universe, which contains orbits, cycles and a vast system of coordination. The explanation of clockwork does fit that mysterious movement. So, we're contained within some huge timepiece, and we see our own seasons and rotations, all obeying metronomic rhythms. That's comforting.

Back to the millennium: Does the clock strike for our little planet... maybe, I should say, does our little clock strike every thousand years, announcing a time for sweeping change, for instance?

"Yes. With every thousand-year revolution, We have plans to change this globe, according to conditions appearing on its surface. If they have developed appropriately, then certain things will be enabled to take root. If that's not the case, then We will destroy the surface of the planet and, either eliminate the planet entirely, or start all over again with a renewed surface."

Could that be compared with farming, in any way? A farmer plows, plants and harvests, and does various other things to a field, according to what has happened to it during the year. A flood, a need for special fertilizer, an earthquake, a blight, or a planned construction project. All could radically interfere with his usual approach to that land. Also, certain basic operations might come according to a long-term timetable. If we look at our little space island as simply a patch of fertile or infertile ground, might this analogy apply?

"Yes, it would. The work due at this millennial timeframe is changeable. It's only a general indication of what's ahead for the occupants of the field. A general clearing off, burning and plowing, is always in the future for every planet. Their written scriptures contain records of past demolitions, as well as predictions of future ones. This is not anything bad or evil, but simply good farm management. And, it will come to pass that each place of living will have its time in the sun and will be given a chance to bear fruit; to become a beautiful and prosperous garden. However, the occupants also have a responsibility to their residence. They must maintain good balance – without causing damage to their global neighbors – or they might cause a blighting of the whole field, as if a fungus had taken over. Earth is in a very vulnerable position right now and We had despaired of any cure, as We've been watching for many thousands of years. Sadly, We had planned a global destruction for this Millennium, if the condition was not cured in time."

So, that's why all of those End-of-The-World prophecies were contained in so many of our religious beliefs here on Earth in these "End Times?"

"Yes, that's why, indeed. Conditions had led to two world wars, just within the past century. A third world war was narrowly averted and the danger has not yet passed. We are watching your planet very carefully in this early timeframe of the new millennium. It's as if you are all on trial for your lives.

But, much has changed in this first decade of this millennium and We assume that things will continue to change for the better. Though the various material and spiritual pollutions appear to still be here, in plenty, We believe that the root causes may have been eliminated. Some current disasters filling your media news these days may be evidence that negative pursuits are being excised from the general planetary life."

What causes such an unhealthy planetary fungus? Criminality of the occupants?

"It could be many things. Negative vibrations begin to outweigh positive ones. Under a microscope, you would see this activity like a cancer, spreading through living tissue, and it can take many forms and affect mineral activity, as well as organic activity. Criminality is different from most human behavior, and it spreads vigorously once it takes root. Even law-abiding humans often behave criminally towards their mineral planet, itself; so it fails systemically. This, eventually, comes as a complete surprise to the occupants who had no idea their actions were so corrosive, and had caused them to become a cancerous fungus upon their own planet."

Wow! You sound like an environmentalist! That's what they've been telling us! But, only within the past few decades...at least, so that we'll listen. What does this have to do with our planet's timing device? With the millennial tick of the clock?

"Everything! Because this period is when We decide whether to pull the plug on the continued existence of the planet, Itself."

We're up for review, right now, then? Does this tie in with the Mayan Calendar, which stopped with the year 2012? Everyone seems to be so conscious of this, even though the Mayan Civilization is long over.

"Yes, it does tie in. Twelve years into the new millennium is but a heartbeat in Our timeframe. However, We watch for signs of hope during the dozen years after a rollover. We are finding hopeful indications of a possible recovery. A new calendar comes into effect around that time, even though the occupants of Earth won't know of its existence for many years and will continue using the present one. We'll be watching your planet during this delicate timeframe. Hundreds of years will pass before Earth's field will be perfectly normal again, but maybe the dangers will not result in elimination. Farmers are always adjusting their fields and hoping for the best results possible. So it is with Earth!"

Oh, my Holy Spirit! So many people are finding it easier to communicate with You because of this new Inner Hearing capacity and They're gaining confidence in themselves, rather than in the old way of religious orders and traditional worship. Is that a good attitude to have about all this?

"Oh My God! Yes, yes, yes, yes! We have been so busy contacting people to find their open channels, and guess what! They are already linking minds with Us!" What do We tell them to DO?" "Nothing!" is the answer! They're already doing it, just by linking minds and words with Us! The rest will follow naturally.

And that's the right approach for any human being. They are on Earth to experience life. Just take Us along with them and keep on talking to Us, like their best lover and friend. Because that's exactly what We are!"

TIME IS AN ENVIRONMENT

Juan Martin Fernandez, Economist, Educator, and owner of two hostels in Uruguay, sat with me on a bus between Montevideo and Colonia. He admires the philosopher Camus, which led to our own philosophizing. The following questions about Time and Space were the result:

What are various ways to measure time?
Do Speeds of Time differ?
What does the Fourth Dimension include? Fifth? Sixth?
Are the Higher Dimensions "dimensional?"
Are there any additions to Time and Space? What other factors should we consider in cooperation with them?
At the Speed of Light, why does Time stand still?
What does Light have to do with Time & Space?
What causes Light? Is Fire always involved?

Oh my Holy Spirit, "Are there various ways to measure Time?" Can You give me a simple answer to start with? We're on the bus and it's hard to write.

"No, I cannot give you any simple answer, but I can give you some really good complicated answers if you will take dictation in a quiet place where we can break down this subject, bit by bit. Then We shall see what We shall see!"

Do You have any suggestions as to the questions we should ask first? These are all over the map.

"You should start with what you know about Time, and that's actually very little. Let's define those terms first, before we go off-planet with them. Martin has a wonderful mind and We congratulate him for being so inventive and inquisitive. We can't wait to dig into this subject with you, but it's hard to do it on a bus. Let's take our Time and give you more Space to write in."

<u>Later:</u> *Okay, I'm an Earthling in a three-dimensional universe. Does that reality place us in a particular, measurable, definable Time/Space Paradigm? Oh my Holy Spirit, is this a good starting point?*

"No, it is not. Let's not consider these other paradigms, because I can hear that next question, waiting to be asked, if I tell you that there are differences. Let's try to answer

"What exactly IS the Earth Time and Space Dimensional Reality?"

"What would you like to know, specifically, because it's harder to answer general questions and We like to go bit by bit, as long as you can understand what We're driving at."

Okay. "For whose sake was the Passage of Time created? For us, the Creatures (as in our life spans) or For Your Own Sake?"

"Now, that is an extremely simple, yet very deep question. I will have to consider that for a few minutes, as it has never occurred to Us, Up Here. Will you explain why you thought of this as your first question?"

We take Time for granted and, in the modern age, have become slaves to it. But that, more or less, is artificial, and it

is dictated by our machines concerning our daily life. That could all disappear instantly in some great catastrophe, without destroying our actual life. Our bodies grow and age; our pregnancies progress; our stomachs demand food and our bodies want sleep– all without any intellectual knowledge or measure of time. Ancient societies used the sun and the moon, plus crop phases, and did very well. So, our "tick-tocking" may simply be frills and furbelows on present-day life. Unnecessary in the final analysis. But, why would Time be any more important to the Creatorly Level, if You simply set things in motion and then wait patiently for the Creatures to evolve at their own pace? In the long run, what difference does Time make?

I'm sorry, Time. You and I are very close and I've never needed to think like this before. But, how, why and where is Time an essential element to Creation?

"My God, Linda Layli! You are absolutely correct here! We have not explained it to you, have We?"

No, I'm surprised that this central subject has been neglected. Thanks for asking about this, Martin!

"Well, you are correct! These things just roll along and they do have mathematics behind them (a subject that you don't understand), and the "timing" of everything is calibrated to the nth degree, but it runs on some Upper schedule that has nothing to do with the *passage* of time, and everything to do with inner sensitivities... the fruit ripens and falls from the tree... birth occurs at various times for different pregnancies, ...civilizations rise and fall according to internal stresses and the behavior of those within. And, nothing is standard! So, no clock sets these schedules! Forthcoming actions are dictated by every individual situation, within an average timeframe, for which there are as many exceptions as there are rules.

Thank you for discerning this! It's one of the dichotomies of all materialism: that **"No one is Minding the Store,"** but so much is determined by the Entity, itself. And yet, there is movement of time, and aging is the lot of all particles in a created realm. So, time appears to rule supreme!"

All right, how do we factor Space into this squishy formula? Do the two terms, Time and Space, always interact together in the dimensional worlds?

"Y.E.S! They must! In order for anything to leave the First Dimension, where you will admit, things are pretty limited: being only a single point, with no depth, height or width beyond its own self. Which is, possibly, where many Third-Dimensional-people would prefer to remain."

Does Time ever "define" the size of Space? Or have any effect upon its size? One of our questions was about when light speed is achieved, that Time is said to stand still. I'm so far out of my understanding zone, right now, that I really can't even understand my own questions. Help!

"My God, Linda Layli! You have opened the door to something that won't ever close again to the human minds that can go there. Yes, that is the truth. Time does define the size of space, and it stretches as the dimensions increase. Have you noticed how, when We are talking about these Inner subjects, there seems, always, to be plenty of time to cover them completely? Or, even that a short answer satisfies that particular point? Time is a very stretchy-sided environment.

And that word says it all: **TIME IS AN ENVIRONMENT!** A quality that is usually only associated with Space..."

Oh yes, and when we say, "Give me time..." etc., we really are talking about space. Usually meaning "Back off and let me think about this. I need more time..." It's really space that we want, but it's the sort of space describing the here and now, in relation to some future point."I'm out of time" means that we are squeezed and can't expand, or wait, any longer! That's why the word Time/Space is often written that way!

ORIGIN OF THE GOD CONSCIOUSNESS – AND WHY NOT A FEMALE GOD?

Karen and Erin, whom I met at Paz y Luz Resort in Pisac, Peru, asked the quintessential question: "Where Does God's Consciousness come from?" Karen was also quite clear that she preferred to call God a "She," rather than a "He." Oh my Holy Spirit, what can You tell Karen and Erin?

"Oh, My Linda Layli, Layli Linda! I don't know how to say anything to these beautiful souls, because I haven't thought about this matter before. I don't want to tell you that I am male or female, because I am neither one. I just am, and that is just that! I don't reproduce Myself in the sexual way, as all of My creatures must do. So, this is the only reason that sexuality exists…other than for pleasure, of course, and We do have love and sex in these Higher Realms. But, it is very different. It does exist. It's just too complex to go into in a short answer."

Karen asks about the source of God's Consciousness: "What created it? How did the Beginning begin? Creation bespeaks a Creator, but is The Creator created?" Oh my Holy Spirit, in pondering this question, I think that I know why I haven't asked it before. I can feel my finite mind stopping short of attempting to tackle Infinity. It's like trying to enter a Black Hole, certain that rationality can't follow; or even words that would carry logical meaning for me. Is it because I have simply accepted the existence of a Creator and don't need the details? Is there any way that a human can relate to an explanation about the origin of The Creative Force behind all existence on any Plane, whatsoever?

"No, I don't think so! There's no way to get from here to there, logically, in any language conceivable to the human mind. And, when people want logical proof, of the scientific sort, We may as well close up shop, right there. It's simply not available, and that is one of the conditions governing the Created Realm that you live in. The mind can't 'get' this equation, but the heart, which can well up with love for an Unseen Force…for a concept taken on faith alone...is capable of that. This is surely why you've never asked this question of Me. You don't need that physical, logical, scientifically-couched, convincing proof of My Existence. You know Me, personally, and are one of the unquestioning human believers. No answer about the Source of The Source exists for this planet! You'll understand much more once you leave the limitations imposed upon Earth's residents. Ask the same question in your new realm, and you still won't receive a more definitive answer, but your ability to understand the answers you are given will be much greater.

Honestly, Linda Layli, Layli Linda, belief is at the core of understanding almost anything. Seriously, the open-minded questing attitude, without the closed-minded "show-me" attitude, is very important. The many powerful Upper Beings, Who are denizens of the God Realm, are very different from Earthly humans. There's not much sense in going into details about Them to those residing upon Earth. In turn, even those Upper Beings don't tread on the subject of what Their Heavenly Creator is made up of. Actually, this is what the word "Mystery" applies to. Many things are impossible to comprehend from a more reduced level. Wonderment is a bridge to understanding, or at the very least, the willingness not to *have* to understand everything before accepting its reality."

As an Earthly analogy, I keep coming up with the word Mathematics, and the miracles that numbers can create. Engineers and scientists, throughout time and place, use the same decimals to do miraculous creating. Ancient Peruvians designed bridges and roads as well as Americans or Australians do now, and their Incan terraces and temples have endured throughout millennia. We all accept mathematics. But, WHO created it? Was it really only Pythagoras? Apparently not, according to Princeton University.

Does it matter to present-day results that we nail the origin down? Is it any less real, if we don't know? Even if we ask "Who is the originator of Math?" and are given an answer, would that name remain in our memory, or even be accepted by the next guy? I'm willing to take my chances that the numbers used to get my airplane launched will also guarantee its safe landing. That "Faith" then frees me to travel widely, just like the not-needing-to-know-where-God-came-from frees me up to love Him unabashedly.

NEWS FLASH! GOD BOTH "DOES AND DOESN'T" EXIST! ALL AT THE SAME TIME!

Now, in the wee hours, I thought of a most original and unasked question, and I'm giving Him plenty of time to come up with a completely original answer. I'll wait until after breakfast to ask it. How could it have already been asked? The Believers wouldn't even have an inkling of an idea to pose it and non-believers would have no one to ask!

DO YOU EXIST? *Oh, my Holy Spirit! Would You like to open now with the remarkable subject of whether You exist or not?*

"Oh My Linda Layli, this is such an exciting question because, amazingly, the answer is both yes and no! Originally, while you were at breakfast, I was preparing all the proofs in the world to convince anyone of the fact that I surely do exist and how could it be otherwise? Everything in existence comes from a source, and without that source, how could existence exist?

"It would be impossible for all complexity to simply spring, accidentally, into place, all by itself, with no plan or coordination. Microscopes reveal the underlying connection of all things, and there are hints in telescopes that this Earth is only a very small part of a great and magnificent whole. There are so many ways to look at this question – and to realize that clockwork needs a clock designer and a painting needs a painter. So, the existence of a single created object speaks eloquently of a creator. What scientist, or atheist, can deny such logic, when their own fingerprints are so individualized among all the fingerprints of mankind? Randomness has never been orderly. Of course, I exist!

But, just as you picked up your pen to write My answer, the thought struck Me, and I heard it registering in your mind as a result. 'How can I exist, because I am outside of existence?' Yes, I do create existence by sending particles of My Consciousness into the created realm, the world of existence... and I clothe them with form, which I call into being from matter, which exists only in these lower kingdoms created by Me, the Non-Existent Being, The Uncreated – Who 'exists' alone and invisible, in My Own Realm!

Even the Kingdom of Heaven is an intangible sphere of being, as opposed to the Earthly Realm of corporeal *existence* and place of life. This Earthly Realm is all about tangibility and I am not tangible. Therefore, by the accurate definition of the very analytical-thinking scientist, I do not *exist*! And, his rationality insists upon the ability to detect Me according to his precise calculations and criteria for the substance of reality. There are none of these clues for him to find; only the traces of the results of My Presence, which are not enough to convince him of My Own Place within creation.

I exist above My creation, but the unbeliever cannot register or quantify that divine scale – and so he names these causes as unknown, thus far, and continues to sift the sand for clues of an original causality. He is correct, and the believers in Me are correct as well. But he is misguided, because he relies upon creation to describe its pre-birth, and no created thing can do this.

So Faith, which is a great intangibility itself, but a well-understood condition not on the auction block of definition; Faith makes all the difference between a believer and a non-believer.

But I tell you this! Any scientist who can register the sound of My Voice and who will respond to it, in the merest of pleasantries, will not remain a non-believer for long. For at last, his physical sense of hearing would have undeniable proof that something, without a trace of visible form, can directly communicate with him on the inside of his closed mind and can touch his own soul with the light of impeccable logic. All he has to do, in return, is to stay honest and unafraid, and to learn the lessons and the answers to his utmost questions – which I will gladly unfold for him. This is all the proof that he will ever need, theoretically, for him to turn into a believer himself.

But, actually, this can become a very unwelcome test for many intelligent humans; and they will often choose to remain in the dark and deny that something completely unexplainable is occurring within their brain, through the agency of their own inner hearing channels. They flee from "this madness" which threatens their own, well-ordered world of achievement.

Such is the way of the world, which I, Myself, have created to be the most intensive test and the most severely blinding factor covering the secret of man's own origins.

So yes, I do exist – and no, I don't exist – all at the same time! It is as it ever has been from the moment that the first created entity emerged from My Own inventive mind. Existence was designed to be a great proof and a great screen of My True Reality! And the answer to this enigma sorts the humans into two different categories.

But, either answer is absolutely and perfectly correct."

IN WHAT DIMENSION IS THE HOLY SPIRIT WHO SPEAKS TO ME?

Abadiania, Brazil: In what Dimension are You, my Voices? Oh my Holy Spirit! Where are You?

"Oh, My Linda Layli, Layli Linda! I'm right here with all of you lovely women. All anyone has to do is to turn, Innerly, and listen to their thoughts, which are My thoughts forming in their own head. I want so very much to communicate with such advanced human beings, but most of them seem to believe that this isn't permitted to them. Therefore, they flee from the idea that words might be coming to them from a dimension high enough to be occupied by The Holy Spirit.

Why should any believing human think that? I've always been the connection between all created things and their Creator. Only recently among people sophisticated enough to organize themselves into religious communities, after I sent down yet another Manifestation of God..."

Pardon me, did You send the Manifestations down, or did God?

"We both sent Them down. That was a very good question, though, because these humans need to divide Us up, according to our roles."

We do like to categorize everything, don't we? Sorry for the interruption. Let's get back to what You were saying about "only in recent history when the religions began to appear..."

"They, the religions, came between Us and every human on the planet! There came into being a priestly caste that didn't want ordinary people communicating directly with God, because that would eliminate the need for an organized religion. But, the Messenger was sent to educate humanity about this very need to speak directly with God."

And we do like to organize things, as well. To make the simple complicated, and to add formalities. Is it possible to pin down The Holy Spirit, or God, The Great Creative Force, to any location? This questioner would like to know what Dimension You occupy? Perhaps that, too, is part of our human tendency to organize things in our own minds?

"We are in every Dimension because We've given Our Consciousness, in proportion to size and function, to every single created being. So, it's possible for Me to be with My Own Consciousness everywhere that it exists. All that's necessary is for that little dollop of My consciousness to turn to Me, wishing to hear My Voice; which is its own voice, ever residing within its own head and heart."

CHAPTER THREE
HUMAN CHARACTERISTICS

HEAVEN'S OPINION OF HAPPINESS

Oh my Holy Spirit! Tisa of Pago Pago, American Samoa, has a question about Happiness. What is Your definition? Are they happy in Heaven? How about in Hell? Is all Happiness the same as it is on Earth?

Oh my Holy Spirit! Here's an emotion that every human knows about and wants to feel... Happiness. But, getting right down to it, what can we say about it? It's very subjective, since different people value radically different things. Yet, there's a common strain of it, which is universal, and which burbles along in the human heart, shining from our eyes or spontaneously popping out in laughter, music or joy of every sort. Animals, especially dogs with their wagging tails and expressive natures, share this trait with humans; maybe in many surprisingly similar ways. Well-being must be a bottom line for happiness. But that definition is elusive, because simply surrounding ourselves with the tools of well-being soon becomes flat and tasteless, and our hunger for that innocent happiness quality returns.

After all, the belly-laugh... a real, heartfelt, unabridged guffaw... is one of the most rewarding and releasing proofs of a pure moment of fun. Pleasure, in its truest and most adult form, is best defined as FUN! So, my Love Above, is that what Happiness really boils down to? Fun?

"Oh My God, Linda Layli, Layli Linda! It is, it is, and it izzity-is-is! Oh My God, Linda Layli! Are We having fun yet? There you are, giggling, as you write this, and We're all busting Our guts, laughing Up Here at your great definitions and your serious exhortations on the subject of Happiness and Fun. That's not anything you usually do before posing a question to Me. But I might have pontificated in My usual way, if you hadn't warned Me away from it.

You're quite correct in everything you say about Happiness and its elusive qualities. "Fun" sums it up pretty well. Fun isn't easy to come by, as it requires a personal ability to completely let go and go with the flow. That's a rare thing for adults to do, which is why fun is mostly reserved for children. And, even they are soon expected to have fun only within approved circumstances; not having much to do with work, religion, education, or any human pursuit in the course of a successful life.

This kind of training stifles happiness, making it available only when the consciousness is overwhelmed with the humor in a situation, or when it leaves convention on the doorstep and is lighthearted enough to make happy emotion a part of daily life. All children start out this way, but too many are sobered up quickly by overbearing adults who've forgotten how to laugh easily and frequently.

We love funny people! Genuinely funny individuals are also extremely popular among their fellow humans. They are happy people. Funny and happy go hand in hand."

Are You saying then, that funny, genuinely happy people can't accomplish serious work?

"No, I'm certainly not. Sometimes, they can do more than the average person could accomplish in two or three lifetimes, because happiness draws help from the Unseen Kingdoms. We're drawn to Earth when someone operates their magical personalities and focuses irresistible attention on something worthwhile. We'll help them in every way possible, and they usually sense that. So, We're back to the bottom line: "Happiness IS nearness to the Upper Kingdoms," a very special joy producer and a marvelous elixir for the human race. Happiness is enhanced when happy souls spread this great form of loving human-bonding around.

Then, in addition to that rollicking convention, there are the heavy-duty vibrations from an alerted Angelic Realm, which then attract ever-ascending Heavenly Levels from way above the solar system. Everything gets downright seriously deranged, as far as the possible joy is concerned. Such happiness usually just goes on and on, settling into a loving feeling that breaks out, now and then, into hearty laughter.

This is what We want Earth to turn into, eventually! Happy people are like little puppies! Warm, fuzzy and willing to trust; to cuddle up and gnaw on just about anything, without snarling or biting each other."

IN DEFENSE OF RIDICULOUSLY SILLY HUMAN BEINGS

This is a continuation of dictation taken in Pago Pago, American Samoa, in October, 2012, on the subject of Happiness and the Human Race.

Oh my Holy Spirit! Wow, What poetic license this subject is bringing out in You! Neat! Can You comment about what Happiness... or a happy person... looks like to the Upper Realms? In addition to their magnetic effect which You just described; what are they, themselves, like, in Your estimation while they're on Earth, and then, when they die and appear in Heaven? Which is getting us back to Tisa's original question about Happiness and Heaven.

"This is a special question which We'd rather not answer specifically because it's just too overwhelming to describe adequately. You see, I, in My greatest Self, the Godhead, from Whom all creation originates, hoped that I would see Myself succeeding when I was faced with obstacles within My solid creation. All of those "given situations," which I dreamed up to fill those universes with. Then, I planted My Own consciousnesses within so many forms living inside of those horribly difficult material situations, practically designed to crush the spirit. Any and all of those situations could have destroyed my inner qualities of Divine Happiness.

This was the Test! Could I survive anything that I might throw at Myself? These happy human beings, as well as all happy animals, microbes, and planetary systems galore, all prove that: **"Yes!" I can, and do, and will, survive anything that might crush the spirit.** It proves that the Spirit is eternal and is basically un-crushable. Even if only a few of my experiments exhibit this loving quality in its most pure form, then that's enough to allow the rest of My creation to catch up to that ideal −however long it might take them.

These sometimes silly, gloriously happy people....

Ever since the world began, I've been hoping for silly humans to multiply! I know that sounds ridiculous and it is ridiculous, when taken literally. But I'm referring to the truly free souls who just don't stand on convention very much, and who love to explore the outer realms of possibility − which most people sincerely regard as absolute foolishness. But they, the silly ones, ask themselves such silly questions, such as:

"What if man could fly like a bird?"

And then, they invent a machine that allows people to do what no bird has yet done: fly while carrying hundreds of humans, thousands of miles, every day and every night, ad-infinitum. The Wright Brothers were thought to be very silly men in their time. The Dreamers. My, oh-so-funny dreamers!

Talk on a cord across the planet? Land upon the moon? What's next in the mind of another ridiculously-silly personality? I can't wait to find out!

Sober-sided people think that I don't know what's in their hearts and minds. So often, their denial of joy, except in their own sanitized, collectively-approved packaging, is so abhorrent to Me that I want to poke them in the ribs, so that they'll ultimately catch onto the secret of Life. It's all about happiness, sincerity and love! Not about rules and common acceptance patterns. Society needs those things too, to be sure, but they should be the result of a loving heart: the loving heart of a mother dog, licking her puppies and nudging them around. Not barking at them to stop wagging their tails so often and getting into all sorts of ridiculous situations.

Chasing a scent to the ends of the Earth, just to see where it leads! You'd better stop Me! I'm waxing poetic about canines again!"

GOD'S OWN ABILITY TO SPEAK DIRECTLY TO HUMANS

Steven recently submitted this wonderful question: Holy Spirit, please tell me how do You speak to me, and what can I do to hear You every day?

"My God! This is the one question that I have been waiting to hear since time began, when all of these particles of the Consciousness of The Great Creative Force, God, were sent forth into the Realm of Created Matter. Beautiful, beautiful bits of His Mind, sacrificially going out, away from the cozy confines of His Own Brain to become the consciousnesses of every sentient being: human, animal and otherwise.

We have never been able to speak to all of them, simultaneously, since then. That day of mass communication has not yet arrived, but it is beginning. The energy is building up for the scattered particles to return to Home Base, and to realize that they are the brain cells of a much larger creative existence than they can ever conceive of, individually.

So, Steven, this is a very welcome question, which has been asked by someone every day since the origin of man; but in a rather lonesome and hopeless way, because the overall belief has been that God does not speak directly into the hearing ear. Possibly, into the heart... but not with clearly understood words, addressing each person's point of reference. This has, of course, happened before and become recognized, in spite of the general denial, but there's still great controversy and personal upset surrounding all claims of direct communication between The Creator and mankind.

Medically speaking, there's no way to prove that you have heard anything out of the ordinary, and this is a great dilemma to those who are convinced that these thoughts... either profound or lighthearted... did not come from imagination. The solution to this particular problem is to focus on the communication and its meaning to you, and not to try to convince anyone else of what's going on within your mind. Carefully, you will come across others who can deal with such vast implications, and it will feel natural to share your own personal experience and learning curve with them.

We are opening all souls in this wonderful, most natural, direct link to a Home from whence they all emerged; but this is going to be a gradual and natural awakening, based upon the wishes of the particles to return to their point of origin. The Act of Will begins with such a question as yours. The answer has been waiting, sweetly waiting, for the impulse of such a question.

"When the student is ready, the Teacher will come." "Ask and ye shall receive!"

So, Steven, My Love is drawn to you when you approach Me like this. That's what prayer is and does. When you have time to wait for an answer, simply become aware of any number of changes: Do you hear any new sounds? Feel any new sensations? Register any new thoughts? Just be patient to receive the inevitable training of your opening inner hearing channels. It may proceed slowly. It may come quickly. Don't let it throw you. We have no purpose but to become comfortable with each other, and we have plenty of time to do that.

What you can do, in order to hear Me, is to give your brain some downtime; to disconnect from all of the stimuli of the world around you, especially these new attractive eye and ear stimulators: computer screens and earbuds. We love these gadgets just as much as you do, as a matter of fact; and they are creating a non-physical, galactic mind within the physical universe. So, don't get me wrong here. You need that and it's the direction for mankind. But don't let it swallow you.

Because here's the irony: You and I must have quiet and privacy in order to commune, down there, deep in the recesses of your own soul. And we deserve some quality time to do that. How you arrange it is up to you! I will be patient, but you are calling the shots concerning your own particle, your own individuated brain cell of The Whole. How, and even if, a person returns to The Center is an act of free will, and that choice will vary, naturally, among the created beings, as it always has. I might suggest that when you are lying down, ready for sleep, that you call My Name or focus your mind in My direction.

I want to say something to everyone here! Do you believe that this is possible? Any direct communication between Me and you? If you do, it will become easy! If you do not, then you are not ready for this conversation and probably aren't even reading this. It really is as simple as that! Either way is okay with all of Us. There's no emergency here. Creation knows its own way. Ironically, it's now only the highly-developed creatures, the human race, who are still outside of this direct-communication equation. The lower life forms, and the animals take Our connection as a matter of course. Scientists call it instinct or group mind.

Can you see where things are heading? Humanity has always been given a choice, and it has used its freedom wonderfully... as well as willfully. It still enjoys free will to decide. But, *"the times, they are a-changing, and love is magnetic, after all."* A call has now been sounded, assisted by a new millennial timeframe, and scattered brain cells are stirring in the warmth of Spring. Welcome to the Conversation!

WHERE DO OUR PRAYERS GO? WHAT DO THEY DO?

Oh my Holy Spirit! Patrice asks: What happens with our prayers when they reach Your Side? Where do they "go" and exactly what do they "do"?

"Linda Layli, these are such original questions that even I don't know all of the answers until I investigate these matters from Up Here. I think that I can safely attempt an answer...."

(Suddenly, there's such an implosion... a vacuum-feeling... in my ears.) What was that I just felt?

"Would you like Me to explain it to you? I Am The Great Creative Force and I LOVE this question so much! Do you know how much I welcome these questions? Please keep thinking up new ones, because this is how the veils between Me and My Beloved Creation become thinner and thinner. Possibly, minds will be able to grasp Me more securely. It's very complicated... this region between myself and the material world where I live within every sort of body, occupying every imaginable place where life occurs: on many planets, under many oceans, in many jungles, cities and deserts. Places where things are very different! However, prayers exist between us, within all of these radically-varied environments.

Call it Connection; Thought Transmissions; or Words, Songs, Hopes and Dreams; Needs Realized and Needs Communicated. All is prayer. It is connection, simply connection! Sometimes, connection has a theme attached to it. When that happens, it's like sending a telegram directly into My Heart. You want healing for yourself or for somebody else; a long-standing wish or desire, and you *finally* get around to imploring for My help – which I already know about, by the way.

So, it's very simple as to what happens the minute you form a prayer deep within your heart, and then direct that message to Me, no matter what form it takes. Maybe you're on your knees; maybe you're lighting a candle, or reading and reciting words taught to you by a religion? Those beautiful prayers, by the way, are only effective for you, if you say them with mindful attention and hold their intent firmly in your heart. Just repeating the words, absent-mindedly, doesn't have any true access to My Mind, at the moment.

It's the heartfelt intent that I'm listening for. When I hear your sincere prayer, I *always* do something, but it might not be to deliver exactly what you ask for. If it will help you or those involved, you might receive the instant miracle you are longing for. Maybe I'll do this by putting the perfect obstacle in your path so that you'll learn the necessary lesson more quickly; or I might see that you are already on your way to obtaining what your life plan is calling for. Or, I might simply love you all the more and arrange for My warmth to envelop you in a fuller and deeper way, but leave the matter of your prayers unsolved for the moment.

It's the *attempt at communication* which prayer provides, that's the true object of praying. When you believe in Me, you pray! When you don't believe in Me, you don't pray! Or else, you use prayer like a chess piece, hoping to prove My existence to yourself; but more easily believing that I'm not a true reality if a prayer does not deliver the goods. Sometimes, I wait and see; and sometimes, it wouldn't be wise to supply what a person asks for. Many people pray for death in order to end their suffering. But death isn't what they need; since only a continuation of life can provide them with a chance to learn the lessons that life is trying, at that very moment, to teach them.

So, to answer your question, all sincere prayers go immediately to the Ear of God. What happens then will be just exactly what should happen in that particular instance. There are many things and conditions that a human cannot know about, behind the scenes. But what *always* results is an outpouring of more of My Love, felt for the person who does the praying and for the object of their prayer. It focuses My attention there and builds up Our relationship. Prayer is always beneficial, because you and I always wind up holding hands.

What I desire most is for you to come to Me with casual, heartfelt words, even when you have nothing to request of Me. Just include Me in your daily, and nightly, life. Nothing formal. Just a cheery, *"Hi Ya, God! I'm doing fine! Thanks a lot for everything! Bye now. Love, Me."* That would make My day, if even a few humans started making Me their New Best Friend. I could get a lot of mileage out of that! After all, I'm the Author of the book that they're writing with their occupancy of my universe. I'm the Architect of this universe, which surrounds them. I would so love to be included in the life they're living within My Creation!

I really don't enjoy being an Invisible Host, standing right here at all times; being so ignored by humans who live in My house. Sometimes, the only prayers I hear are demands or complaints. Many want maid service, when they're perfectly capable of doing something themselves.

Think of Me as your gracious host, and treat Me as politely as you would the owner of a lovely mansion where you are a guest. Talk to Me any time. I give you free run of My house and grounds, but sometimes you'll find Me looking after things or checking up on your welfare. Please don't slam your door and deny My Reality. I'll be your good friend, if you'll let Me.

We could make a game of leaving notes for each other, stuck in the garden wall, hidden in a secret place...however you feel comfortable connecting with Me. I'm not so high and mighty that I'm inaccessible to all the human guests in my beautiful mansion, this Earthly planet, and all the other celestial spheres where I also make My residence."

PRAYER FEELS THIS WAY FROM THE OTHER SIDE

Let's talk about the effect of prayer. How do You define prayer? What is it?

"Prayer is like a tremendous light force, especially when it's applied with sincerity and gusto by one of the spiritual giants on Earth. Its effect on the Holy Kingdom is instantaneous! It can not only bring about results, but it also adds to the quality of life throughout existence. It's a huge and driving force, which most people can't appreciate.

Prayer is not the formal formulas that many people think it is. It doesn't require any particular posture, place, or time of day. It is beautiful beyond measure when it comes from the heart and the soul of the person praying. The most sincere prayer has the greatest effect. Prayer is communion with God, or His Manifestation, and it isn't just one-way. Prayer isn't just words coming from the person on Earth, but the hearing of Words from God, in answer to someone's conversation with Him."

Two-way prayer? Can people literally "hear God's Words," as You say?

"Yes! They really can, and they can hear the Words of the Messengers of God when they pray sincerely to Jesus, Moses, Mohammad, Buddha, Krishna, Baha'u'llah, or any other Manifestation of God. We cannot say how well anyone might register these Voices, because they are heard within your own head and they sound like your own thoughts. You see, your brain is your only receiver, and you are accustomed to hearing your own thought processes. So these Answers might simply pass for your own thinking.

It depends, also, upon your spiritual practice, so that your mind can concentrate on Me and be open when I do speak. Many distractions take place, which dilute My Answer. One of the most common is that whenever the person finishes speaking to Me, he just closes up the prayer session and goes about his business and doesn't expect to hear anything in reply.

Life is very understandably busy, and I can't get your attention once you have closed off that little room where you go, mentally, to communicate. I'm often the only One inside, waiting to say My piece, when you finish letting Me know the contents of your heart."

IS A HEAVY-MATTER REALM IMPORTANT TO SPIRITUALIZATION?

The following is a quote by The Holy Spirit from my book, IN SECRET DIFFUSION, speaking about Spirituality:

"It is essential to live in this heavy-matter realm because the process of spiritualization causes you to become the opposite of what you are. You must become lighter and lighter, both in spirit and in actuality, though your weight may not change. Your molecules expand in some way and are more loosely-tethered than the molecules of those who are unspiritualized. This is of great advantage in the levels of higher vibration.

We don't see how anyone on an intangible plane of existence could go through the struggle necessary to bring about his own transformation. Each soul must *break through*, from one condition to another, and no one can do this for anyone else. Think of the qualities of love and enthusiasm, a spark from within. These spiritual traits cannot be manufactured and cannot occur where there are no choices – where triumphs can't be known because there are no obstacles. To know the Spirit and the Soul, and to know that the Upper Realm has a powerful influence over the created realm, is a true triumph when achieved from within an obviously material existence. This must be done where the two forces, the Upper and the Lower Realms, can intersect.

Tangibility is a part of creation, and it functions as a means to hold the spiritual existence during the earliest basic level of development. Every individual needs to conquer, through personal knowledge and experience, any fear of being contained in an environment that is not completely manageable by his own willpower. In the non-tangible Upper Realms, one's environment and the objects in it prove much easier to control and to use, simply through the force of the mind.

In order to spiritualize, it is necessary for the individual to become securely attached, through his inner nature, to a Holy plane of existence that is invisible to him. It's as if your bodies and your surroundings provide a sheltered place for your spirits to retreat and to venture upwards. This instinctive groping is like a plant's leaves and tendrils turning towards the sun, even through the dark forest or from under the soil.

Once you leave this physical enclosure, you go into a state of consciousness without any physical individuation and you lose the ability to "go within," or to push against something solid, in any attempt to abstract yourselves from your surroundings."

AMONG DIFFERING PSYCHIC INFO, WHICH CAN WE TRUST?

In New Zealand last year, I met a lovely woman who had many psychic talents, and who used her ability to counsel people through reading their auras. We had long conversations about each other's work in metaphysics. She was interested in knowing how I could trust my Inner Authority when I pose these questions.

Oh my Holy Spirit! Valerie wonders about the Authority of Your Voice and how to tell it from the various ones that she consults, which are layers of her own persona – her consciousness, her aura, her soul. These give her distinct and individual answers: "Yes and No" indications, as well as degrees and years, and she learns much through her own system. She wonders why we need to consult such a large and diffuse Source as Yourself, when our own bodies have good knowledge to reveal? Would You like to venture a comment upon that conversation?

"Oh, My Linda Layli, Layli Linda! Thank you for asking Me this question. It is one of the most important considerations for any human to face: <u>*"Where do you turn for your guidance?"*</u> Many people do not turn to any Sources, other than the physical/material ones which give them the opinions and discoveries of their fellow man, some of whom no longer live in the present era. These multiple sources are the only influence for the majority of Beings living on the planet. They cannot ask questions of this inert printed answer.

Oh my Holy Spirit! I know that this question actually and specifically concerns psychic advice, which usually isn't identified with the religions of the world. But, You mention "Guidance," which is associated with the revealed religions. So many people do get guidance from their formal religious faith. It's just not what we now refer to as psychic. Is that the difference?

"Yes, it is; and no, it is not! When We say psychic guidance, We are talking about something that is sent specifically to individuals living on the planet, at that very moment. This was true, also, of the Revealers of all of the religions. Their Words were written down, as received, and filled volumes of Holy Revelation that later became the foundation of a formal religion. None of these Prophets and Revelators made those words up! They came from God, just as the modern-day psychics receive Word From God when they ask a question, either on their own behalf or someone else's behalf. So, the Revealed Writings are also among those that I was referring to.

Oh yes, people have added to the sciences and the general body of knowledge, and there is wisdom in these discoveries, and those who consult such Halls of Records are the educated classes whether those records deal with spiritual knowledge or practical, physical knowledge. Even the spiritually-advanced individual must know many of these Sources.

Then, there are the inner avenues of gaining much knowledge and insight by psychically- opened channels, such as Valerie has learned to do. This is very effective, and she is good at what she does and has worked out her own ways to converse with these portions of herself, which are in touch with unlimited levels of inspiration, as well as distinct and actual records pertaining to her question of the moment. There is really no need for her to venture into other regions or sources for the knowledge she needs to access in order to help her fellow human beings. She works sincerely and effectively to reveal problems in the background of humans who still struggle with ancient and recurring relationships, and her information sources are adequate for the questions she asks. In fact, I would not be working on similar problems, nor interested in accessing those particular archival records. So, I couldn't help her to achieve those answers. It's apples and oranges.

What you and I do is not the same, at all. So, there's no need to weigh one method against the other, as there is simply no comparison. That said, I may well try to contact Valerie sometime through her open channels to the Upper Regions, because she has advanced far beyond the ordinary humans that I described at the opening of this answer. But even if we were connected in the future, as We are now but subconsciously, she would still need to rely on her bodily system of gaining that sort of information when she wanted to investigate helping someone, as she is doing now.

I only work in vast dimensions and large-scale ideas, and I watch the human race as it learns how to incorporate these spiritual avenues into their ordinary information-gathering techniques. In fact, those answers which you have published in your books and blogs will amplify those written accounts to which people turn to get their present information about spiritual topics – and that is one thing you should be doing to help the human race to elevate its own spiritual understanding. Each one gives according to the talents that they have cultivated within their lifetime.

This is the hour of the maturity of the planet, and many levels are engaged in bringing this about. So, Valerie's recognition of her own individual levels and the unique talents they bring to the table is a microcosm of what your planet must learn to do. It must access all of its own considerable talents, heretofore latent within it, while expanding its consciousness far beyond its wildest imaginations to realize its place within the cosmos. To do this, it will, gradually at first, and then, more confidently as time and practice allows, begin to relate to ever-higher dimensions.

It is this opening to its higher potential in the spiritual realms which will bring Earth to fruition and maturity in the company of those of whom it is not yet aware. As the rare individuals on Earth awaken to their own communicative abilities, so will the entire planet profit from a new connection to its source of being. Earth is not considered to be a high plane of existence at this time, but it has great potential, and it is beginning to stir as these individual human consciousnesses make their connections to higher powers. Just as the overall quality of love is spread around, one heart at a time, to benefit all and to elevate the atmosphere of love over the whole planet, so is the prayer and consultation level able to rise as more and more Earthlings practice their own comfortable style of contacting the invisible realm in an everyday and lifelong habitual way. It has a dynamic effect upon the atmosphere that surrounds their place of life – ultimately spreading and enveloping their whole planet.

So, one way is not necessarily better than another. Each is appropriate to the mission embarked upon. Hopefully, all of these methods will join together to elevate every level of the body of mankind, as a whole."

ARE PSYCHIC TALENTS ALIEN TO PLANET EARTH?

The ability to hear and see things that others on the Earth Plane cannot hear or see became a curiosity to me when my psychic talents opened up in my early forties. The following is a part of a conversation I had with The Holy Spirit about these matters: People who have psychic talents must struggle with the knowledge that they are different, especially as their talents begin to make themselves known. Oh my Holy Spirit, can You comment on the successful ways to cope with this?

"Yes. Don't worry about it. This is perfectly normal. The presence of these talents indicates that a person is one of the highly-spiritualized people of the Upper Kingdom, who has come to Earth for a special reason. If they take care of this trust, I will reward them with My Presence during their lifetime."

Are these talents, in a way, alien to planet Earth? Or are they lost conditions that we used to have?

"Yes, I have been trying to raise up a group of friends, down on Earth, who would spend time talking to Me and who would ask Me questions and write down My answers; and who would entertain Me by letting Me look through their eyes. I have found a few but not very many, out of all of the spiritually-talented people whom I have sent to Earth over the millennia.

Now, to answer your question. They are not actually alien talents to Earth, because I have provided many humans with these features. You could say that they are lost conditions, because during other times around, there were very many of these spiritualized people on Earth at one time. Far more than now. Most of those people used My gift in a much more responsible way than during this present cycle, when the psychics have badly abused this talent."

Are all humans potentially psychic?

"No, not even potentially. Though some psychics say that all people are potentially psychic, it's just not so. Most Earth humans do not have these capacities. And that is just that. They cannot take lessons to encourage a talent if it's not naturally present. The psychics were not sent down to make everyone psychic, but to connect the two worlds. The people who have become the customers of psychics do believe in this other world, but they shouldn't have to pay such fat charges in order to learn these things."

Then a psychic ability is a condition of the next plane of existence, chiefly, and not here? Do those who exhibit these abilities unconsciously leak them while they're here, living in a material human body?

"Yes, these are all natural parts of being in the other world. They are nothing special there, in that everyone can do these things. I don't think that these talents "leak" so much as "standout," when found on a physical plane of existence."

Do You have any advice for people who have psychic talents that give them an extra edge of information?

"Yes. Don't use these talents foolishly. Use them for the benefit of humanity as a whole by letting Us talk to you and to others through you.

"HOW IN THE HELL DID I GET HERE?"

Self-Realized wrote: "I want some help. I'm unable to focus on my studies and I always get distracted to new dimensions, other noises and natural technology, to work for and heal this whole planet and to raise vibrations of humans. I have many plans and ideas. But, at present, my higher studies are also important and I must complete them for further research, as self-help to my satisfaction. I can see my aura color, a purple color whole. Only, in daytime, it looks like green and blue. Any information will be very helpful. I'm female, 23, preparing post-graduation in the engineering field. I await your suggestions on how to be more focused, rather than becoming lazy by either procrastinating or turning to distractions. Any ideas please? Thank you very much for this blog."

Oh my Holy Spirit! We're in a noisy little cafe here in Lima, Peru, but can we take some dictation on this good question on how to be more focused and concentrate on serious studies when there are so many distractions... perhaps caused by this student's higher-dimensional talents?

"Ohhh, My Linda Layli, that question is not what she really wants to know! I don't quite know how to explain what she really...."

(Ouch! There's a big soccer game on TV in this tiny restaurant) Okay, let's begin with Your telling me what her real question is, Oh my Holy Spirit!

"What she really asks is: "How in the...."

Was that H.E.C.K? or H.E.L.L?

"It was Hell. 'How in the hell did I get here? I must have taken a wrong turn somewhere Out There. Why did I wind up on Earth, of all places?'

This is a Holy Being... a really, really High-Dimensional Being, Who has come down here to do some emergency repairs to this "Hell Realm" of a planet, and she has suddenly found a way to squeeze a question in an Upperly direction. She'd like to know how come she can't do those same things that she could do Upstairs?"

Did the purple aura give her away?

"Y.E.S! She knows who she is, and she's puzzled by the green and blue aura, which is her daytime outfit. She'll be happy to hear that everything is all okay, and she won't have to worry about her productivity. She might feel a lot like a traffic signal. No sooner does she get a good dream at night, in her purple stage; then she wakes up, reduced to green or blue, and there's just not the same oomph in that. So, all the nighttime plans get ramped down."

What would happen if a Purple Aura person wasn't disguised down here on Earth?

"They wouldn't like this place at all. By being green or blue, they're protected, a little bit, from the skinlessness that higher individuals feel down here. We're always amazed that *you* can take these vibrations as well as you do...."

So funny! Because, tonight, in a loud, crowded Peruvian 20x50-foot café, it's so full of noisy vibrations! But, they're good ones...because Peruvians are such good people.

"Yes, but it IS hard to function, spiritually!"

It's hard to "hear" You. But, the hostel is noisy too. My nose is so itchy! Is that You, Basing?

"Y.E.S! It's very difficult for Us, but it is a perfect place to answer this particular question. One thing is for certain sure: This Being is well-equipped to do what she came to do. She cannot fail! She's perfectly safe there! Tell her not to be so hard on herself. It's okay to take her time. She's very, very smart, so her studies are guaranteed to produce her desired results. She's permitted to relax, and enjoy herself, if she can possibly consider this assignment as a vacation to a funky farm region where people in her situation almost never have to go. But, here she is! Still young, with possibly many years ahead for her here. Tell her to: 'Just enjoy the farm life! It will have its compensations, as well as its great, upsetting discouragements.' And, not to be too sad that her dreams cannot follow her into waking life. It won't be long, in relative terms, before she can get out of here and prepare to elevate, even beyond the purple scale; for being so brave, generous and talented to do a tour of duty in this dirty, old planet, way down here on Earth. Tell her this for Me:

'You are helping to elevate all things – and it will turn out to be worth coming down, in the long run!'"

IS POSSESSION REAL?

Kat has asked about Possession. This could certainly affect both sides of the track within the Upper and Lower worlds. Can You cover the co-existence of disembodied spirits as they relate to the living?

"Yes, I'll be glad to. First of all, We cannot concern Ourselves with how the current population feels about these matters. Mostly, it's simply unknown and not a topic of concern in today's world. Sensitive people may understand that spirits exist, which can attempt to use the bodies of unaware humans for their own devices. Sometimes, these sensitive ones can release the human from such an influence. Many times, the affected human can help himself. We have already discussed this many times, over the centuries, and your own book... Our own book...*In Secret Diffusion,* covers this quite well.

A possessing spirit has become enamored of an Earthly life and clings to the Earth plane, instead of moving on at death. It seeks a living human, usually one attached to the same desires that they had in life; and thus, tries to continue its material dependency. Neither being has awakened to its true reality and recognized that there's much more to existence than the lower material realm.

The solution is for the occupied one to seek the help of God in throwing off his tormentor, and to become responsible for the course of his own life.

COULD CONSCIOUSNESS ALSO BE A MAGNETIC FORCE?

Oh my Holy Spirit! Could consciousness be referred to as a magnetic force?

"Y.E.S! That's exactly what consciousness is! A magnetic force! How did you get to that conclusion?"

Well, I imagined the creation of a human, beginning with a mere slip of a small bit of Your Consciousness, which is the creational starting point of all of us. Then, I thought of the molecules of matter, which must immediately become attracted to that new human. That's a magnetic act, right there. Growth is a form of magnetism when nourishment flows in and enlarges the original matter.

From the moment that this gift of consciousness stands alone, it ATTRACTS material for its use. During all of our life and our passage through time, things flow into our hands, whether we are aware of that, or not. We use those elements to build everything else upon, assisted by experience and education. Then, we match the resulting influx with an outward flow of creativity towards other magnetic consciousnesses that are living around us in the form of society.

This magnetism moves us about through life, interrelating with others in ways that would probably mirror magnetic particles on a flat surface when viewed from high above. Watching New York City traffic from a position in the sky confirms this supposition. When our magnetic intake and outflow ceases, we become inert and can't function in that ever-interacting realm; so we're removed, perhaps to begin afresh in a completely new stratum of magnetism, on a brand-new dimensional table.

That higher stratum, and our role in it, could well be determined by the charge that built up in our consciousness when we existed within our original assignment. So, this is an informed magnetism – and it is possible to create it from the purely natural one with which each human is originally endowed.

For instance, many people go through life, simply reacting to their circumstances and letting emotions flare up because of what has collided with them at that moment. An attractive potential mate brings up passion and possession. A threat to person or property brings anger or aggression. Primitive responses are like a match struck on the side of its box, and the resulting fire can be hard to control. This is the whole story for many humans who don't realize the magnetic forces taking place within their own being. In the worst cases, life becomes a train wreck, because they've made no attempt to control that magnetism at their core. It has become spiritual road rage.

"Yes, and this is how karma is an energy force that can be consciously shaped by every human being; just as a talented energy worker can use the natural magnetism within each human's consciousness to bring creativity and an outpouring energy gift to the humans circling around every living being. This can affect the ongoing future of nature, as well as human society, and can change the direction of individual consciousnesses –bringing them to higher levels of service within the whole of creation. Energy can be stored and built up. This is the power of magnetism and magnetic force. It's a great battery – highly-charged with love and giving – rather than smashing and taking."

Is this the direction that each of us should strive for? To contribute our energy outpourings to that great collective battery?

"Yes, it is!"

Wow! It's a perfect description of nuclear fusion, which I've been praying for, for so long! Maybe when You say our planet is not yet ready for fusion, instead of what we have now –

dangerous nuclear fission – You're actually saying that humans haven't built up their personal inner capacity to give and love sufficiently enough to charge our own planetary battery? When we do that, then we will have created a new energy source for our planet...the far-superior, cold, nuclear fusion! So, it must be something that You cannot (or will not) bestow upon us, undeserved, but is a condition that we must create for ourselves?

"Yes, that's it! That is the magnetic power of love. This is the karma that your friend, John Metatron, of New Zealand, was undoubtedly referring to. It is the love, the positive magnetism, which will so radically change the future (karma) for this planet.

We, in the Higher Realms, hope and pray that your little magnetic consciousnesses can bring about this transformation on your own planet, and qualify for the new energy source. You, Linda Layli, have been praying for this since the year 2000, when you first heard that two sets of scientists, in two different countries, had simultaneously achieved cold fusion, often called nuclear fusion, in a bottle.

Can Earth qualify? The Upper Kingdom judges are holding Their breath, hoping that enough of Earth's human magnetic particles will use their new love energies productively and spread this life-changing power to your planet, which direly needs some human intervention, right now."

IS MODERN TECHNOLOGY CHANGING CONSCIOUSNESS?

It's late March, 2013, and I've been traveling alone around the world for eight months now; staying always in dorm beds in hostels. In a cute hostel named The Pickled Frog in Hobart, Tasmania, Australia, I made many friends in their twenties. They spoke of the changing landscape of human behavior, which now includes handheld devices, such as smart phones or small computers. They, too, notice the silence that always characterizes a collection of strangers, now focusing on gadgets instead of each other.

Mela'ni, from the U.S., wonders if technology is moving with, or against, our consciousness, both individually and collectively? What is the direction of humanity? Phillip, of Germany, asks whether having all choice has eliminated our ability to choose?

Do we now stand frozen and immobile when faced with almost too much information and too many possibilities? He feels this in trying to decide upon a career. How can this come under control for us? There's so much immediacy, and need for action, that he feels fear of making decisions, because it puts limits upon his endless choices. Do we spread ourselves too thin with all of this modern technology at our fingertips?

Oh my Holy Spirit, my hostel mates are all concerned about the same modern-day changes for humanity. Where is all this technology leading us? Especially that which provides us with attractive and endless time-consuming opportunities? Or maybe, I should say: endless opportunities to consume time? What's the best way to adapt to that which is already bombarding us?

"Oh, My Linda Layli, so many times I have wanted to address this question – but there doesn't seem to be a point in consulting with humankind because this isn't really an issue with them yet. My God! This is the New Era that's washing over their heads and it has simply poured in since the Year 2000. It will seem to overwhelm this generation for their whole lifetime!

For one thing, they remember the past and can compare these radically-different time periods. But, one has only to look back a few decades to the period before electricity; then, the days before telephones, TV, and now, computers. So far, everyone has smoothly incorporated these conveniences into daily life, and would consider themselves paralyzed without them. Phillip and Mela'ni are children of these computerized gadgets, which open all kinds of doors for their generation: these twenty-year-olds. The fact that they're feeling overwhelmed now, with this cornucopia of knowledge, just beginning to flood your human possibilities, is evidence of the speed of change, particularly in this past decade. Now, how can I help them to deal with this?"

"TAKE COMFORT, CHILDREN!"

(The Holy Spirit is repeating this phrase in a higher and higher, more excited range, so that I can barely hear Him. We're doing this dictation in a rather noisy hostel common room.)

Okay, You are telling them not to worry. Let's focus on Mela'ni's specific question: "Is technology moving with, or against, consciousness?"

"Technology is challenging every human's consciousness, as it requires a new level of focus which hasn't been necessary to develop, heretofore. Earth society is still under-developed, in comparison to many other galactic societies. This first blush of technology must train primitive Earth brains, so they can become acceptable to higher societies within the cosmos. These are the early steps. Similar to an alphabet being taught. Many new concepts are coming to the aid of this very generation. Tell them that they're still in nursery school, as far as the complexity to which everything will explode within their lifetimes."

So, Phillip's concern that too many choices and opportunities will result in complete inability to choose, is simply an inevitable, temporary phase of the new millennium's mental conditions? Is that correct? That temporary brain freeze will take care of itself?

"Yes, it certainly will! This is, again, an entirely new crossroads, and people will soon sophisticate and learn to maneuver through the confusing maze of great opportunities. It is a problem of more advantages, and ultimately, that's not a problem, at all.

These young people's children will not complain about these same things!"

WHY DO HUMANS HAVE A HUNGER TO FIND A MATE?

One of my fellow hostel guests in the Hostel Hanging Gardens of Babylonia, in Montevideo, Uruguay, asks a very good question, basic to every human heart. Prem, of Holland, wants to know:

"Why do humans have an innate hunger within themselves to find a mate? Not just anyone, but The One for them?"

Prem had just said goodbye to a man she'd known only for a few hours of conversation; but both of them felt that they had "known each other before in some other life." He was returning to Europe; she had just arrived from Europe to settle in Uruguay. Chances are, that without deliberate planning, they will never meet again in this lifetime. With such a limited time to get acquainted, much had been left unsaid which might have opened the door to future communication. Neither had confessed to the impact that the other one had made; so no addresses were exchanged or hopes to stay in touch admitted. Soon, it was time to say goodbye and that was that! I found her still mourning this loss of new-found hope, in the hostel kitchen, chopping vegetables for dinner.

With tears, she asked about this bewildering sort of attraction. I told her that she had just met an Intergalactic Friend, (an IGF); that it always feels this way; and that, even if neither speaks about it to the other, it rakes both, equally. It's always mutual and it's very, very rare. I promised to take dictation on the question of:

Why, now that Prem has felt such an impact, will she always hold out for an IGF- quality mate?

"Oh, My Linda Layli, Layli Linda! When you are taken Up Here, We will tell you all about this IGF Phenomenon. Meantime, with everyone you talk to about it, when they feel it, you have taught them how to love and to listen to their "Angel of Love," inside of their sternum bone. This AOL will not come out, and will not even stir or awaken, until she finds one of these special, special people whom she recognizes from many associations on the Upper Level. She, your Angel of Love, is usually so disappointed that she can be terribly sad if she has to say goodbye soon after meeting one of these special, special human beings, whom she has already known and loved in the Upper Kingdom."

The kitchen became busy and dictation ended, so I'll continue this definition by quoting a few excerpts from my chapter about Intergalactic Friendship in my book, In Secret Diffusion.

"They are people whom you have known instantly, every time you have met them, throughout every one of your lives. That is all that it is: recognition of old friends! And, you feel just like you always did towards each other. It's just that, in a new lifetime, you both know that you have never met before, and so, you think that it's something somewhat supernatural, though it's actually the most natural of all friendships."

Is this Love At First Sight?

"Yes it is and no it's not. If the circumstances are right for falling in love, that might happen – and then it would be true. But, these individuals meet you in so many different forms and often are not eligible for a personal, loving relationship. Many are already married, or their age is too far from your own. It doesn't matter to the instant friendship, which always forms; but *"ships passing in the night"* is the usual description of these Intergalactic Friendships. There is nothing planned for you to meet, at all. So, it's completely random and that's why it's so very precious, each time it does happen.

Let's say, hypothetically, that I met an available man who proved to be an Intergalactic Friend, and we formed a long-term, sexual relationship. Would the attraction remain at the initial high level, or would it settle down and become dulled over time, as many ordinary relationships tend to do?

"It would remain very powerful all of your lives. These relationships are old, long-time relationships, which don't diminish for eons of time; so they are the ideal partnership for a marriage or a long-term friendship. It's just that they are hard to find where circumstances are favorable for staying near each other. It's magical when you appear together on one planet at the same time – so magical, so unexpected, and so special!"

Should we hold out for marriage to only an IGF?

"No, that's impractical, though I know that's what you have done. Having tasted this kind of unity between souls, it's hard to settle for something less, and the tragedy of being bound to another, if you should meet an available IGF, would be awful. It's impossible to know if you ever will meet an IGF with the right combination for a marriage."

Is it safe to say that we have been in love with an IGF sometime earlier in our evolution?

"Either as a love partner or a best friend. There are different kinds of IGFs. You usually can recognize the type, and you both fall back into the old routine, automatically. There is, essentially, no estrangement on either side. So, yes, you have been very close in the past."

Will we ever meet them again?

"Yes, you will! That is in a Dimension to which you all are heading, destined to spend forever together. Maybe not all at the same time, but these are the companions who are coalescing to be associated forever in the Realms Above. It's like a training course that you're all going through, which leads to the same ultimate condition."

And so, Prem, now you know why this chance meeting impacted you so powerfully. Had you been in the hostel the previous two weeks, as I was, you would have had plenty of time to get acquainted with this lovely man. As it is, you were "ships passing in the night," and your heart hurts because your little Angel of Love (AOL) got her hopes up, upon the unexpected meeting of an old Love. She's tucked into your sternum bone, and that's why you ache to hug that stranger. His Angel of Love lives in his sternum, and they urge the two of you to press your chests against each other for their sake. When that doesn't happen, those two will grieve until they finally fall back asleep; not to waken until the next IGF, of that same lover-quality, comes along. Once they know how this feels, they don't take too kindly to the ordinary garden variety of Earthbound lovers.

But, whatcha gonna do? This occurrence is so rare and so delicate, that if you can be a little bit bold and give the friendship every chance to survive; then the four of you (that's including two AOLs) just might get to live "Happily Ever After!" It's certainly worth trying it if you should ever recognize this powerful phenomenon again. Things may not happen instantly, because your meeting is like a bowling ball dropping on your heads; but it's worth all the time and attention that it takes to nourish that sweet happenstance. Just remember that it's always mutual!

DEVELOPING INNER HEARING ABILITIES

Hot, hot, hot and sunny. I'm in a little Fijian park on Waya Lai Lai Island, waiting for Eliza to arrive for a lunch date. Last night, my dreams were deep, and within them I met up with Brad Pitt, who was supposedly the Pope. I offered to go get him some food???

Oh my Holy Spirit! Eliza and I have finished lunch, and we are talking about her dreams and messages from Above. Do You have any general advice to help her develop her inner hearing abilities?

"Oh My Linda Layli, yes I do have some specific guidelines, and what you have told her to do is just a little bit wrong. She must not try so hard to connect with Me, because it will be her downfall. If she wishes to talk to Me, let her sleep a lot, sleep a lot, sleep a lot; and relax a lot, relax a lot, relax a lot. She is not being tested by life. She's testing herself, and that's so hard for her. We don't want her to be so hard on herself. Every now and then, she will relax and something can get through, but it's okay if nothing comes through right away, because she's very talented, both psychically and spiritually. We don't have a bomb under her but she's trying to whip herself to perform – and We want her to take time to smell the roses. Okay, read her this much and see if she has any questions about it."

How does this hurrying, or tension, affect her present health and hormone balance? Any advice?

"I know that you will seek a competent doctor, Eliza, because this Upper Business is never any substitute for physical medicine and its solutions. We can't really diagnose anything physical, unless We're the Ones Who have caused it, and I don't think that applies to you. Okay, I don't think it's too serious. One thing that helps Linda Layli is to trust Me completely, and she does that to the nth degree. But, she's a happy Being, who hasn't got anything wrong with her. Part of the reason for that is that We have been intimately connected for a very long time – and she's so willing for anything to happen to her that she doesn't worry about the outcome.

So, try to learn to "Trust In The Lord!" as all the churches and all the religions and all those Who come to Earth from time to time to tell people what to do Down Here on Planet Earth, say. Just trust and then chat with Us as you go. No formality, just you and Me, jawing away about anything at all. I like it when you, Eliza, talk out loud and don't really have to hear My reply. I mean, don't stop your conversation to hear My exact words, unless that feels natural. Just get in the habit of "Talking to yourself," whenever you won't be overheard… and that's just so people won't think you're crazy. You can write things down like this, when my inspiration comes through, in order to keep these things to refer to, if you feel comfortable.

Just remember: no rules. Be easy on yourself. It's going to work out!"

HOW CAN MANKIND DEVELOP A NEW COSMIC CONSCIOUSNESS?

This is not a direct question/answer exchange from The Holy Spirit, though I will ask about it soon. It's a post I'd like to share with you from my blogsite, www.heyboomers.com, about a big experiment that's being conducted by some scientists to create a temporary greater consciousness to encircle our planet. So, here's some background information from my Hey Boomers blog and my journal to prepare for questions to Him, which will soon follow as I participate in this experiment.

It was the most interesting feeling, last night at exactly 11:11 p.m. on 11-11-2010, to lie in bed and pulse my consciousness upward, in order to meet with a vast number of strangers' brains, in probably the most cosmic experiment that's ever been conducted on this planet.

Some scientists and mathematicians, at www.newrealitytransmission.com, were aiming for a million souls to simultaneously connect, telepathically, for exactly eleven minutes somewhere in the stratosphere above Planet Earth to pray for her, or to think good thoughts about her; in order to dispel the murky shades of doom and gloom that humankind's present snarky attitudes are projecting. We worry way too much; we get road rage at each other; we flagrantly soil our nests; and in general we abuse our planet and each other.

The idea was to project positive mental sonic rays out there and simply fizz those dusty, negative projections into nothingness, while experimenting with this undiscovered power within ourselves. At least, that's my take on their intentions, and it was my intention while making contact. They left the purpose pretty general – except that it was to be clearly positive and beneficial for this planet of ours. Now, scientists that they are, these lovely experimenters will be watching for results, in whatever form they may appear.

Okay now, how did it FEEL to me? Oh yeah, I loved it! I lay down in bed at 11:00 p.m., ready to sleep but watching the time on my cell phone, so that I could keep my eleven-minute date with thousands, or millions, of us who were also eagerly awaiting our connection moment; none of us ever having done this before. At least, I have communicated telepathically sometimes, and I talk all the time to The Above, so I figured the same mental muscles would be employed. In the few countdown minutes, I sent my brain groping about, out there in the Cosmos, trying to hit the stratosphere just above Earth. I could feel the pull within my head.

Then, as I watched the digits on my cellphone flip to 11:11, my head suddenly felt funny and not as I had expected. There was a heavy flatness, as if a sheet of iron had been gently placed upon my consciousness. One second, it was not there; the next, it was! Hmmmm? I waited. Then it began to loosen up a little. It was still heavy and muffling, but it got a bit warmer, and I started to catch whiffs of phrases, like little prayers for the Earth. Nice little sayings, which I can't remember now, were floating by, actually disappearing before I heard the entire line. I figured what had happened was that all of us had signed on at exactly the stated moment; and now we were feeling the very same way: "Now what?" There we were, frozen in the doorway and able to sense the rest of us as a new weightiness within our brainpan! It was quite a nice feeling to register that split-second moment of arrival. This weird sensation reminded me, somewhat, of how it once felt to take part in my remote Chiropractic session between Hawaii and Florida.

As our new reality transmission became more familiar to the mind, things relaxed with all of us and I began to visualize my prayers and hopes for humankind and our lovely blue globe. Thinking like a space being, instead of an Earthling, I knew her to be my "home planet," and found the deep affection of one who is away, looking back, nostalgically. You don't take things as much for granted from that perspective! I prayed that The Holy Spirit would be with each of us, individually, as our minds pulled upon each other, drawing something inside of my head upwards and towards the top, in a very visceral feeling.

Long ago, cottage cheese was made by holding a cheesecloth filled with milk curds in your hand and squeezing. Okay, last night, my brain was the curds and there was a feeling of that hand, grasping the bunched-up cloth, tightly, creating a definite pull at the top. That's the best way to describe that eleven-minute communication feeling. I liked it –and I am going back tonight at exactly 11:11 p.m. because we're meeting like this for eleven nights, through November 21st. Hopefully, word of mouth will swell the crowd.

Please do join us, won't you? You may find your sleep a little ragged later as you get filled with the wonderment of it all. No, your brain is not being invaded by bad things. Forget that! There's zero possibility of mental invasion here, if that's what you're wondering. But, it's just so exciting to be a part of this cutting-edge.

January 19, 2015 – Four years later, while organizing my blogs in preparation for the manuscript of this book, I've learned of Neale Donald Walsch's worldwide plan for an Evolution Revolution (www.evolutionrevolution.net) to bring about a new, underlying, positive planetary belief to change our current negative, fear-based systems. Instead of telepathy, we harness the power of the Internet in the hands of everyday people desiring to transform the energy surrounding this planet into optimistic positivity.

Hearing Inner Voices: The Dead Pet Whisperer

ARE HUMAN LIVES SCRIPTED?

Are human lives free-form, or is there some thought that goes into their design? Do we plan scripts for ourselves before we return to a life on Earth? Many studies indicate that we do. I covered a bit of this topic in my book, In Secret Diffusion, but a new question occurred to me the other day.

No doubt, it was spurred by the scriptwriting that I'm engaged in for the Warner Brothers/Amazon.com site, (http://studios.amazon.com/users/10660.) Many times, I'm aware of my own dabbling in a movie character's human life, particularly when it comes to throwing obstacles in their path and making them work harder for the payoff. Hmm? If it occurs to me in my almighty position of power over a fictitious character, might that be true for all of us concerning our Higher Level? I'd better ask.

Question #1: Does Anyone Up There ever decide to equip our individual life with the proper elements of drama?" Say, by supplying antagonists, crises, challenges and/or opportunities, at various points in our lives?

"Wow, you have touched upon something original. Much of a person's life is not scripted, but you are asking about the elements that We "salt" it with, aren't you? This is a good question, because no one ever expects that a human life is actually Someone's Storyline – or could be, if they did something remarkable with everything that's sent in with them. In many cases, nothing distinctive happens and the person winds up living life as a dull individual, more or less crushed by the circumstances that were put in their path. Those are not always negative influences. Sometimes, they're very, very beneficial: such as plenty of money and comfort, or goodness knows how many wonderful opportunities. A human can be damaged by these, as well, if they become greedy, hateful, jealous or resentful.

Anything is possible when one is Up Here, watching over the lives of human beings. Sometimes, We do everything We can to personally intervene and help an individual's life pattern. At least, We try to. But I can't do anything, anything, anything, if the person doesn't believe in God or in prayer. I can't do anything to help him. Like moving his props around or sending in reinforcements or re-writing the ending he's written for himself. As you know, in fiction or scriptwriting, rewrites are always possible until the time that the story is too far along for that. In the case of a life being lived, there's also a cutoff point for intervention; and that's when the person closes himself off to the possibility of higher dimensions, which can, and will, assist him.

Actually, it's like a writer's contract with an actor. *"Will you be amenable to tweaking? Yes or no?"* Many say no. There are medical things, for instance, that We can tweak, a lot, a lot, a lot. But, people do their own surgeries upon themselves, with about the same degree of success, as if they gave themselves a heart transplant. However, they wanted to go it alone, so We let them."

So, are You saying that: before birth, each one of us is put into a sort of a shaker containing many elements and personal qualities? In there with us are many characters and situations, both good and bad! Then, we all get cast out upon the storyboard of life to take our chances? And, from that scramble, we can create whatever we like. Or we can, basically, sit in the pile and let the pieces leak out all over us, doing what they do and writing what they will, upon our nice clean storyboard....?

So, each person has the unspoken invitation to consult with their "Dice-Thrower," who could, if invited, start playing the game in partnership with them! But, if left out, that Instigator must simply watch the game unfold at random. Is that what You are saying?

"Yes, that is it. That's a good analogy!"

CAN PEOPLE WITH DIFFERENT BACKGROUNDS GET ALONG?

This question, from my son, Randy Brown, concerns class differences. Is it possible for people in dichotomous circumstances to get along harmoniously on deep levels, without any horrendous emotional revolts coming up to fracture things between them? Are there inherent, irreconcilable differences between humans based upon race, nationality, religion, economic and educational levels, intellect, social standing and other similar factors, which are obvious variations within the human race?

"No, there are not any barriers apparent, except their acceptability to Me. This one little qualification is what separates the sheep from the goats. No other qualification is really insurmountable between members of the human race. This is so important, this acceptability to the Holy Threshold, that it will divide people all over this new millennium.

I do have information of a general nature regarding some things close to the Earth –particularly, things that touch the lives of those to whom I Am very actively drawn by their own beseeching. It's not always good to share everything I know with humans who are involved with tests intended for their lifetimes. That would make it difficult for them to navigate according to their own decisions. But, if someone is turning towards Me and beseeching the Source of Being; then I will help to guide them to the right "muscle-building doorway." That's how human beings need to work their way through this physical realm of existence."

What a perfectly simple truth! You say that it's the quality of the response within each human heart that's the one basic, and only, important feature of a human being? How each person relates to You determines his ability to harmonize with others. So, two humans who independently love and connect with You will be able to associate together harmoniously, no matter what the trappings of their lives?

Any other combination, whether it concerns someone who is connected and someone who isn't; or two who are not connected; those combinations could fail at any time. Is that correct?

"Yes! That is the simple equation, and it's the determining test for all of My creatures. This millennial crossover was the doorway to a new condition. And there will never be another period of crossover exactly like it. Many of My creatures will not be accepted within the new condition and are falling by the wayside if they're not connected to Me in their central core. Not just in their outward appearance. They will self-destruct in this lifetime, whether that's apparent to those around them, or not."

Are You saying that, if people of different backgrounds have solved the ultimate goal for every life –to become firmly attached to The Creator through The Holy Spirit – then they will be free of conflict with their fellow human beings?

"Yes, that is true. The situation is that the connected ones are so relatively rare that their example is not commonly seen in this plane of existence, where conflict is still the rule. When there's no conflict, people don't take note; and harmony is often never even recognized as an unusual occasion. But it is unusual, and I do notice, and that's the only time that it matters.

I observe My beloved ones as they proceed through the minefields of life. I experience the pride of a parent when these particles of Myself successfully complete life without having become besmirched by their fellow man and the behavior of those who have no idea of Me and My Standards.

This is a whole new transitional period for Earth's population. Tests are going to be very severe for the foreseeable future, while the impure ones are disappearing. But it will be a fine time for those who are taking their inspiration from The Holy Spirit."

HUMAN FEAR...OF SNAKES AND OTHERWISE

I'm aboard a speeding bullet train between the northern coastline of Spain and Madrid, with six hours of unbroken, slightly swaying and a bit bumpy time to take some dictation. Lori asks about the human fear of snakes, but I'd like to expand that to cover the general topic of fears, of all sorts.

1. Animals, birds and insects share this characteristic of fear with us, as they flee danger or defend themselves when alarmed.

2. Fear is a primitive instinct, a base emotion, directly wired into the nervous system, which releases chemicals into the bloodstream when triggered.

3. Even anger is a higher emotion because it relates to a target, while fear can simply be the perception of a threat or an incoming danger. Anger is a strong reaction, with an outgoing energy of defense. Fear can be subtle and diffuse, but anger is often violent and concentrated because it's the force employed to strike fear into the heart of that which frightens you.

Okay, now that we're in the mood to name the beast, let's begin with Lori's comment about public opinion and the media's tendency to fan the flames of hatred for snakes, and to a much lesser degree, of spiders, scorpions, sharks, and such. Naturally, this attitude makes for good headlines, but beyond that, there's the physiological explanation, that humans do feel defensive. These threats are dangerous and can sometimes kill you! So can rabid dogs, grizzly bears, auto accidents and cigarettes, but we don't vilify them the way we do the snake. Lori seems to be asking whether there's a metaphysical reason that a snake itself will cause such a visceral reaction within perfectly intelligent people. Someone with a snake phobia panics at the sight of a non-venomous King snake; just the same as when they're faced with a King Cobra. However, not everyone has this autonomic reaction to Snakedom, and some folks actually enjoy handling the smooth, muscular body of a moving reptile – even the poisonous or constrictor variety – if proper precautions are observed. In those people, the abhorrence is absent. I say this with confidence because it's true of me, as it is of Lori. We like snakes!

So, the question comes down to why humans polarize on this issue? Secondly, would any educational campaign do much good to change those who instinctively fear these slippery creatures? And third, do Biblical references, which equate snakes with evil, lie at the base of this fear? Oh, my Holy Spirit! What is Your take on this knotty question?

"Oh My Linda Layli, Layli Linda! What a great question this turned out to be! I'm certain that we can exonerate the Bible on this issue, because many who can't read, or who've never been exposed to these particular Holy Teachings, are desperately afraid of snakes. It's actually a very tempting literary device to use something for which most humans display an innate fear, as a symbol of that which they are instructed to avoid. So, putting evil in the same category as a snake will certainly help to scare people away from activities that might otherwise attract them. It's the same as personifying forbidden negative traits with a human-appearing devil."

And it's much more likely that we'll run into a snake in the course of our life than we will a fire-breathing Mephistopheles. Maybe a few people will think of the Garden of Eden when they meet a reptile, but not many. Come to think of it, Eve wasn't afraid of the big snake in the branches of the Tree of Good and Evil, but stuck around for a personal conversation and even took a bite of the apple he offered. That story is really about Temptation... and yes, the avoidance of smooth-talkers and slippery agents...but, it's pretty subtle on the fear factor. Okay, are there any cosmic clues concerning the division of human emotions on the snake question? As in, do we come from different parts of the universe, for instance?

"Yes...okay...right! We don't really want to go into this statistical detail, which does divide the human race. Not right down the middle, by any means whatsoever. Most people on

Earth hate snakes. Period! End of question! And no amount of learning is ever going to eliminate that uneasiness at the pit of their stomachs when put in the same room with a reptile. Pure and simple, it is something that they are born with, and it actually applies to about 99% of the population of this planet.

Reptiles are considered alien species, and there are a few humans with reptilian characteristics who are here from other planets, as a result of colonizing experiments that We have conducted in the past. These people would, naturally, not be afraid of snakes. There are also other people who have no fear of snakes because they are from the Higher Dimensions, living on Earth in human form and performing various tasks for Us."

Shall we just leave the snake lovers to figure out where they may fall in those categories?

"We don't want you to exercise caution in the asking of your questions, but sometimes they do give away more than We intended to reveal. So, let's just leave it at that."

IS THERE A FEAR ELIMINATOR?

The vast subject of Fear was introduced by Lori's question about Fear of Snakes. Now, we'll examine many fears that humans fall prey to. Oh, my Holy Spirit! Would You like to address the general topic of fear, itself? This is so much a part of existence, and we haven't examined it, at all, in this cosmic questioning.

"Actually, fear is a basic instinct in all creatures as an important protection against many dangers faced by those living in a material realm. Parents know this as they teach their babies to live long enough to learn the reasons why you don't poke metal knives into electrical sockets or jump into pools of deep water. Fear of such consequences doesn't usually cause a lifelong fear of electricity or of swimming, but occasionally could produce that, with the right combination of dramatic mothering and an overactive imagination."

Then, when we become adults, we spend the rest of our lives overcoming our fears through education and simple maturity. At what point can a realized human let go of most of their fears; or will they always need a basic amount to get along down here in a material realm?

"I would say that they can reduce the intensity of the word "fear," and describe a proper level of emotion, as simply "caution." It's not necessary to fear poverty in order to do everything you can to avoid it. Prudence or caution in your economic life should be enough. You don't even have to be a cautious driver to be a safe driver. Ultimately, fear cripples and caution hampers. When one becomes self-confident, especially when that is based in spirituality, then this will eliminate most human fears.

That's because one admits to a Higher Power, which is very much involved in the material plane of existence. When that happens, there's a deeper level of safety felt by such a believer because he has a recourse not available to those who feel completely alone in the universe. This is a huge fear eliminator."

HOW DOES BONE-JARRING, WINDOW-RATTLING MUSIC AFFECT ITS REGULAR LISTENERS, MOSTLY MALE TEENAGERS?

This entry was written November 21, 2012, in Pago Pago, American Samoa, in the South Pacific. I had just been subjected to a two-hour local bus ride between towns, during which the blasting sound coming out of the speakers was truly bone-jarring. Otherwise, I never would have thought to ask such a question. The Holy Spirit's answer is absolutely amazing, and I certainly wish some medical researchers would check it out. Is there anyone on this planet who suspects that this is happening to their next generation? Here's my journal entry:

I have an Earthly subject to ask about, so I guess I'm running out of Cosmic Questions. Maybe the answer applies *only to Earth and might fall into the human addiction category? It came to mind while I was being victimized by this trait aboard a bus on a long ride home.*

Oh my Holy Spirit! What about humans who deliberately surround themselves with the highest volume of music, either in their vehicles or their homes? I'm talking about those sound ranges that cause solid matter, such as wooden seats, to vibrate underneath you and that thrum so loudly that windows rattle in their framework?

"This is something that has been studied by Us for a long, long time. They are always male, aren't they?"

Yes, I'm quite sure that's true.

"It's wonderful that you have asked this question. Because this subject is something extra-ordinary. Loud music is very common and very popular among males in many different countries on Earth. It's also chiefly produced, played and recorded by males, as well as consumed by them. Do you know what it does to the testicles, Linda Layli? It fattens them and it makes them feel good while they are listening to this vibrating music. Once in awhile, a man or boy under this influence will take himself off into the woods, but will not be able to pee normally. Then, he'll begin to lose sensation in his whole lower anatomy. This will only happen a few times, now and then, but it indicates some cellular changes taking place in the reproductive organs. Naturally, a listener's ears are massively affected, as well, and they will usually become deaf after too much exposure.

Basically, humans are doing this in their youthful years in order to create pounding vibrations upon their whole skeletal structure, especially their seats and lower body. Their bone structure reflects and conducts those intense sound vibrations and that creates a mild sexual stimulation. The public is, apparently, completely unaware of this, and these males get away with sexual titillation, right out in the open. Women never catch on, either! The men usually enjoy this harmless secret. Harmless is what they all think, anyway."

But this practice is lethal to certain body cells, which cannot take this vibration. These are the sperm of those Male Human Experiments. Heavy sound exposure either sterilizes them, or so damages their sperm that their children will be born with defects. Massive sound vibrations are just too much for the liquid inside of the sperm cells; yet that very vibration is what these young men value and seek out!

This is a terrible addiction to afflict any population, and these men will never understand why their sperm count is so low or why their children enter this world with such a wide range of deformities or grave illnesses. We've been watching this reality, which indicates the end stages of a certain kind of civilization, in which males, even before they are fathers, sacrifice the next generation for their own limited sexual satisfaction. Thank you for asking this 'Trivial Question.' It's one of the signs of moral degeneration in today's world on the Earth Below."

Wow! And by the time any of a sound-affected-man's babies are born, the cause is so far removed in time that no one could connect the heavy metal music habit, even if it was still continuing, with a newborn who has a heart defect, or any deformity whatsoever. I just read yesterday that there's a high rate of unexplained heart disease here on this remote South Pacific Island. Remember, I rode a very loud public bus, just yesterday, right here on this island.

Yes, there it is: Samoa News, November 20, 2012, page 15:"For the past week, LBJ Medical Center has had their swing ward set up with a triage station, exam areas, and sonography rooms, in order to evaluate children with a wide variety of cardiac problems: most notably, <u>those acquired from rheumatic heart disease, which affects many children and young adults in the territory.</u>"

Any comment? Is that the sort of defect You mean? When the baby looks normal but something is wrong inside?

"Y.E.S! This could be! Since technology has provided more ability to surround themselves with sound, things are progressing, exponentially."

How about the same sound, not surrounding or vibrating the body, but entering only through the earbuds of portable players – for men/boys and women/girls? I never see grown women, and very few grown men, using these small personal players; but many, many teens are plugged in.

"Well, this is a new development, only about a decade old. Inevitably, sound carries throughout the body. Medical science routinely uses sound to treat or diagnose conditions deep inside of the entire physical system. The person is not aware of the passage of sound waves through their cellular structure, so that's why it's very insidious."

Particularly, I think of fetuses, embryos and babies with a mother, who either feeds on that atmosphere; or who is powerless to escape it herself. Feasibly, the new human could be exposed to this unnatural, torturous condition from their very first moment of consciousness, of conception. How does this affect such an unfortunate human being if they make it into life?

"We don't have any statistics on that. It's so rare and unlikely that they'd be born normal, however; even if the sperm that formed them in the first place was unaffected. Soon, body cells will change, simply because the application of intense sound waves on growing cells is extremely dangerous. It creates an "accident waiting to happen." This is the stuff that lab rats are exposed to, and most of them do not carry their babies to term. Other things impinge, and spontaneous abortion occurs. We do know that sound exposure changes the composition of body cells, but this is a very uncertain field right now on Earth, and it's still too early to predict.

However, rises in Autism rates are probably attributable to this proliferation of self-imposed sound dosage by the younger generation. It's usually the teenagers who indulge in this habit, just when their own sexual organs are beginning to mature. Put two and two together and what do you have? An ever-decreasing intelligence; an addiction to noise, rhythm, and chaotic behavior in younger and younger children; an inability to concentrate or focus attention! Definitely, there is a correlation!

Maybe Present-Day Rome will self-destruct from the inside out?"

ANY COMMENTS FOR THE ATHEISTS & AGNOSTICS?

Oh, my Holy Spirit, do You have any comments for the Atheists and Agnostics?

"Yes, I do and no, I don't! On the one hand, I would probably be a member of their club. On the other hand, they don't believe in Me, so how can I talk to them? I think that we really are united, once you take away the odious interference that religions have plagued them with over the millennia.

Atheists have the right to be Atheists! That's how I set things up in the first place! Nobody has to believe in Me, or in anything else, for that matter! This is a Free Will Universe and anything goes! Of course, that means that everyone takes his chances and must learn to live with the results of his decisions. But, they should be completely free to form, and to live by, their own conclusions.

Religions have done many good things and have been the source of happiness for countless numbers, but they can make life pure hell for people who disagree with them. That destroys free will, so that turns Me away from their closed-mindedness. If religions could only relax and not be threatened by someone else's opinion! Let Me tell you something! I don't even want to get started on this point! Atheists are choir boys, compared with people who perform certain venal acts in My Name. That's why they turned Atheists in the first place!"

How about Agnostics? Are they just junior Atheists?

"I think they are. So many of them want desperately to believe in something, but they can't find anything tasty on the long table spread with every religion's offerings. Nothing appeals to them, but they do believe in Me. They do, but they don't dare articulate it. This name, Agnostic, is a word that gives them a refuge to hide behind. They are not saying that they don't believe in God. They are just leaving things up in the air and holding onto a shred of hope that something may come down the pike to explain things in non-material ways.

Meanwhile, both Atheists and Agnostics take comfort in science, don't they? At least, that's a bird in the hand.

"Let Me tell you something! I love these Atheists and Agnostics! I love their purity of mind, and most of all, I love their independence and their free will, so much! Tell them that I said: *"Hello! Come and have tea with Me sometime! I'm hanging around you all the time because I love your refreshing look at things. Carry on the good work!"*

Ever since I can remember, I have identified with these acid-based protozoa, who dissolve all sorts of fantasies spun by those who see things according to their own design. There is no room for any free-thinking within many of these ancient constructs. I call for more fresh air to come flowing in the portals of the world's monasteries, so that we can all have a part in the exploration of God's Truth. Myself included!

ACID-BASED PROTOZOA AND ATHEISTS?

I'm hostelling in Santiago, Chile, South America, and having great conversations with friends I meet along the way. This topic is a continuation of a chapter in my book, In Secret Diffusion, *concerning Atheists and Agnostics.*

Last night, I talked with Kelly, of Texas, a research scientist working on the southernmost island of Patagonia. She said that she's an Agnostic, and maybe, a full-blown Atheist. I described The Holy Spirit's reference to Atheists as *"acid-based protozoa,"* and we wondered what that term might mean? Especially since acid and alkali (base) are polar opposites. However, I figured that they probably served to dissolve the pompous theories of the Power Force Fields of the planet, the "organized religions;" which Kelly says she can't stand. I'd already told her how much The Holy Spirit loves Atheists and Agnostics. But, of course, until she accepts the existence of The Holy Spirit, she can't really appreciate these remarks. I'm going to ask about this:

Oh my Holy Spirit! Will You clear up our questions about what are acid-based protozoa and what do they do?

"Yes, I will. But you won't be able to be silent about this, once you really understand it, because of the Atheists and the Agnostics. Which Kelly surely is! This concept is one of the secrets of today's world, when Power Force Fields, the Religions, control the minds of humans who desire to be believers in Unseen Forces. The religions do have their share of services to this population of awakening mankind. But then, they've also done terrible, terrible things in the Name of The Deity.

Not all Religionists are correct in their assumptions about the Upper Regions. Unfortunately, these assumptions form the greater percentage of the human belief system. Formal religions put themselves front and center in the administration of all qualifications for entry into "Heaven," and they consign non-conformists to a non-existent place called "Hell." Many of these hard-nosed priests and believers will eventually find themselves occupying their own imagined Hells – simply because those were created by them, and rigidly exist, solely in their own minds.

Now, as to the designation of atheists, or doubters, as acid-based protozoa, I was just using that term loosely to describe an agent that dissolves the foundations of something appearing to be solid but which is rotted-out at the base. These religions are old constructs by this time in their history, and they've fallen victim to the involvement of many human egos since their founding by a Messenger of God, who was a legitimate Manifestation of God. This deterioration of truth does occur, inevitably, over the centuries, as priests and administrators attempt to spread and perpetuate the power of an institution. Naysayers, such as atheists and agnostics, hold up to minute examination any religious institution's illogical arguments and faulty reasoning. They refuse to bow down to any golden calf!

Doubting Thomas objectors, however, are also poisoned by their narrow views, and they, too, die upon the points of their own swords. Such rationalists ignore the truth contained within the beautiful scriptures of every religion. These revealed writings do offer proof of God, and evidence of a reality beyond life in a material realm. So, merely scientific thinkers can't make the leap into the unknown, any more successfully than can materialistic leaders of the so-called spiritual institutions that the atheists hound. Neither group has the necessary equipment to do anything but toy with words and concepts about realms far beyond their ken. They become locked in eternal opposition – one just as flawed as the other.

But, I cheer for My little Acid-Based Protozoan Team because, at least, they're intently curious and they do sincerely seek for truth. It's just that they, too, are closed-minded and prejudiced concerning the unknown, forgetting that science faces the unknown every day. They're in love with physical forces and deny anything that can't be measured or weighed with their own, necessarily limited, factual experience.

Both camps do advance humanity's progress, but they're also obstructionists who tend to cancel each other out. I leave them to their own devices and focus on humans who are not unduly influenced by either one. Open-minded seekers with discernment and unfettered imagination are not too easy to come by on this material plane of existence; but when I find such Beings, I try to feed them a lot of information and as many clues as I can get through the filter of their resistance. Little by little, their doubts subside and they become attuned to My way of thinking. Then, I can share with them the secrets of the Universe, to whatever extent they're able to hear them.

I'm hoping against hope that they will neither fall victim to my acid-based protozoa, or to the inflated egos of the planet's official "spokesmen for God," who would be nothing at all if I hadn't sent their particular Messenger to Earth at some point in history."

ACHIEVING HUMANITY'S OVERALL BENEFIT

My friend, Pablo Sosa, of Montevideo, Uruguay, asks: "What task must human beings now conduct for the overall benefit?"

"Linda Layli, this wonderful question is too long just for Me to write it in one session. It's not just one task.

Can we lay it out and organize it?

"Yes, I think so. Let's see... where to begin? What We are doing now...because We have had this new millennium...We are trying to jump-start a new beginning. But, We have so much *CLEANSING* to do first, and much of it is being done on a planetary basis. Haven't you noticed these economic disasters and crazy weather patterns taking place in many civilized countries – yours, in particular?

These are simple methods of washing away the debris of the past, and until this process completes and things are rectified, there's not a lot that any human individual can do except to improve their own spirituality. Crisis usually brings out either the best or the worst in human hearts. So, My advice to every human being is to have more and more and more faith in God, and simply hold My Hand while the vacuuming is taking place. This was a warlike planet that almost slid into the forbidden Third World War status. It must be scrubbed clean, and that is always a harsh procedure. So, those who would be here to help Me rebuild must now take care of their own spirituality, and grow as close to Me as their life's vein.

I want them all to listen to My Voice inside of their heads, and to respond to it privately. This is a radical departure from what was known as prayer in the past millennia, and many won't be able to do this out of fear and self-preservation. They will continue following an outdated standard. But there are humans who can make this switch, free from ego and an all-too-human desire for power, and they can show Me that this planet is redeemable and already has inhabitants capable of working with Me instead of living only for themselves.

I will begin to work with these "Listeners," and will help them to survive the rapid changes of these End Times. We will make a new world with our happy conversations and heartfelt, mutual love. You know what, Linda Layli? That does about say it! It's not as complicated as it sounds. I want to talk to more people directly, just like we are talking now. How do you feel about this prospect?"

Wonderful! I'm always hoping to find others in which this is also happening. And, I went through my own "She's crazy!" days, and I can assure anyone else that this is really possible and valid – and safe to incorporate into a life. So, the short answer is:

- *To Trust*
- *To Turn Upwards With Love.*
- *To Listen*
- *To Respond*
- *Privately,*
- *Personally,*
- *Naturally,*
- *And not with formula, ceremony, or other people's words.*

Right?

"Linda! This is what you *have* to get across to humanity! That's it, in a nutshell! You are repeatedly telling people to abandon their old practices and come into this new way of the new millennium, leaving the old forms behind. So many people who can hear your meaning, who are even plugged in enough to know what you are saying to them, are already leaving these ancient ways behind them. They know that, somehow, the old practices have "lost their salt." But they are not yet daring to think that their own salty thoughts are the ticket to Me. I want to tell them not to turn away! I will protect them from the negative forces, which are now being scrubbed from this planet!

Who do they think they're hearing in their sleep? I love to talk to them in there, and I Am impatiently awaiting their waking response! We have a lot to discuss, and the more human beings who will trust Me and this process, the faster the human race will recover from the cleansing necessary at this turn in time. I need open channels. So here's what My Lovers can do for Me now: *TURN, TRUST, and TRY IT ON FOR SIZE!*"

CHAPTER FOUR
STARSEEDS

COMMANDER ASHTAR SHERAN, OF THE INTERGALACTIC FEDERATION

<u>John of God Healing Casa in Abadiania, Brazil,</u> - I was completely unfamiliar with this topic when Yves, of France, posed his query. It's taken a long time to finish the dictated answer, but it seems to apply directly to the four of us who are temporarily living here now: Yves, who asked this question a full month ago; Elena, who saw a spaceship in the sky, in Slovenia, during her girlhood; Edielson, our Portuguese teacher, who also saw a spaceship above Brazil during his youth; and I, who wish I'd seen one too, but haven't yet. Oh my Holy Spirit! Who is Commander Ashtar Sheran to the four of us?

"This is Commander Sheran, of the Intergalactic Federation! Each of you has been called here to discuss the future with me. I commend you for heeding the call to arrive in Abadiania, Brazil, at roughly the same time. That test was passed very neatly! The odds against it were enormously great, though things don't seem so difficult once an objective has been accomplished – especially unconsciously. It speaks of your devotion and your talent for the work you've been chosen to do. You have attended this meeting from many parts of the globe, and you still would have missed the significance if Yves hadn't asked his question. Edielson's arrival had to have occurred in the same week that Yves asked…on November 6. It took this whole month to learn that there was a connection between the four of you!

Okay, this is the crux of the matter! We don't have much time left to wait and watch! Today is the 9th of December, 2011. You will have scattered again when the Year 2012 begins. It doesn't matter where you are on the planet, as long as you are sensible and are engaged in the work that you came to do. Some of you know exactly what that is. Some may still be sorting that out. You'll find yourselves impelled into these perfect tracks, which won't be so difficult to understand, after all.

Trust the process! It's the same Force which, so dependably and accurately, brought you four together at this crucial preparatory time before the beginning of the twelfth year after the millennial rollover. The first dozen years of any new millennium, plus the initial zero year, 2000, the bridge year, is the crucial span in any new time period. Especially in reference to the survival of...not only the existing dominant species on that planet... but more critically, of the civilizations present at the millennial rollover. Both of these conditions were in serious danger during the latter half of the Twentieth Century on Planet Earth.

Two world wars had decimated much of the population of a number of countries; and a third world war seemed to be a distinct possibility, up until the last decade of the former millennium: 1990-2000. That's way too close for comfort, and the danger is not yet entirely eliminated. It won't be completely cleared up, so that the Federation can declare the space around your planet again safe for normal surveillance, until many current realities are permanently disarmed.

As you've been told, a third world war is a terminal planetary condition, which is not allowed to continue. Such planets are putdown, or executed, in order to control and contain their contagion.

Congratulations to Earth for maintaining peace during this always-crucial, dozen-year period past the opening of the new millennium! Your long-term prospects will be even greater once the end of 2012 is gained, and the planet has still not engaged in a recurrence of a world-engulfing war. Everything that peacemakers can do to bring about love between individuals constituting their ever-shifting governments, and representatives of the opposite political philosophies, will be a constant improvement of the light value which can nudge Earth away from the self-destruction towards which it has been careening for several centuries now.

Ever since war became the reflexive choice of your world leaders – towards achieving their own personal goals of power, wealth and control – the planet has been more and more compromised in its overall ability to function as a member of its greater galactic society.

The role of a planet within its own solar system, and by extension, within the vastness of its assigned galaxy, is usually not the concern of the individuals living out their relatively short epochs upon a planet's surface. However, mankind has chosen a course of aggression towards its own self; like a being who eats its own limbs, or a mother who destroys her children. This is an abnormality within a dominant planetary population, and cannot continue indefinitely. The monster must reform of its own accord, or it must be eliminated, so that it won't spread the cancer of disunity beyond its own self.

At the same time, however, mankind does have an excellent inner, spiritual nature when that's allowed to flourish; even though these qualities have been powerless to overcome the evil of selfishness and the darkness of ungodliness represented in the population as a whole. Rather than religious avenues, which have also found temptation in warfare, the powerful capacity for love towards an unseen Creator remains a possible saving grace for Earthlings. This quality has always existed, but not within a numerical majority of the population.

We want everyone working on the surface of the planet to keep their minds clean and clear of the things that are going to start boiling up in the news. Have you noticed how shallow and foolish the quality of world news has grown lately? The Internet has encouraged degeneration of hard news, and now features only selected, sensational, gossip-filled tidbits about celebrities; into which category all world leaders have fallen. Stories are weighted equally; whether they cover an unusual animal, a horrific crime or traffic accident, or a decision by a political body that might affect millions. In a very short time, the public has become mesmerized into reading only the most curiosity-inspiring and entertaining quips, and they're jollied into believing that all is well.

This is Oz, which has been foisted upon people everywhere. The most civilized populations are the most easily duped. You'll see a spread of this effect as more information comes through personal computers and handheld devices. It will substitute for information, which used to be taken seriously and was well-understood by thinking people. Now, every story is produced in the format of a tasty biscuit delivered onto your news plate in sound-bite quality. To learn more, one must look everywhere, usually finding only more small biscuits of later-breaking developments, with perhaps a few photos. Frequently, a human-interest story might be thrown in, to add a personal touch. All too often, this substitutes for real information, and soon, the topic disappears forever in the constant wash of fresh sensationalism.

The human race has been cautioned about extreme superficiality, which will become the fate of certain information systems. Earth has fallen into a stupor where everyone is addicted to instant information – particularly their own role in it."

We would all agree with your description of the odd mix of stories passing as news on these habit-forming computers, which pander to our idle curiosity. What does this have to do with the way the human race needs to conduct itself in the year 2012?

"We don't have any answers to give you. This is a new dimension, and you're on your own! Be careful not to get lured into the zombie state that the new computer gadgets promise. Don't get lost in cyberspace! The Twentieth Century didn't have to contend with this problem; but it is an insidious way to damage your personal thinking capacity. Not every threat comes in the shape of a nuclear weapon! An utter uniformity of mental tendencies can be much more debilitating in the long run.

Stay awake! Keep your brain exercised and anchored well in the sphere of reality. Don't look for entertainment and distraction. Stick with virtues that have always served mankind! An attack on a planet can begin with simple hypnotism. Just be aware of this and hold to your plan."

Oddly, it was during the Second World War that the term "Brainwashing" was first coined. We imagined the enemy tying a blindfolded captive into a chair and reading subversive literature to him until he cracked and switched to their side. Yet, within a hundred years, commercialism has brainwashed most of us and created willing consumers and restless entertainment junkies, totally dependent upon our electronic devices. Ideology itself boils down to an attractive delivery system: shortened, sweetened, and redesigned to appeal to the masses."

Oh, my Holy Spirit! What do You think of this exchange?

"My God, Linda Layli! You've gone, lickety-split, into an area of great concern to all of Us. Information is a good thing, if it's valid. There's much excellent material on the Internet which has put knowledge in human hands, destroying old boundaries caused by lack of education and solving the difficulties of disseminating new knowledge. This creates a confusing flood, which results in "brain freeze" and total distraction. Ashtar is zeroing in on the main challenges of the Twenty-First Century, which must be approached before too many years are wasted:

1. How is Discernment to be cultivated?

2. How will Creativity be kept alive in the face of instant satisfaction?

3. How will the subtleties and beauty of language be salvaged in the face of convenient shorthand already appearing, such as texting?

These questions haven't even occurred to most people and seem trifling, compared to the intensity of geographic changes which you will soon be contending with. This subtle front can erode your societal foundation if it isn't tended to by intelligent and creative leaders.

Lightworkers have been sent to assist the souls of mankind to survive the challenges they now face. The fact that many of these challenges are self-induced... war, as well as petty pursuits destroying the intellect, doesn't excuse the human race from finally getting down to the business of elevating itself to qualify for advancement into Higher Dimensions."

ORION'S AND THE PLEIADES' EFFECT ON EARTH'S POPULATION?

I met Ethan Law in Cusco, Peru. He and his girlfriend, Taylor, have a very strong connection with the Constellation Orion. He wondered whether Earthlings come from these heavenly bodies, or do we all originate upon the Earth? So, let's see if we can find out how our Earth population relates to such far-off star systems. Science hasn't defined them in relation to living beings or planets; only by the brilliance of burning, celestial bodies visible in the night sky. Scientists refuse to discuss any connection that we might have with other dimensions. Neither do we hear of human consciousnesses, now living upon Earth, having originated within these remote, yet physically visible, celestial territories.

Well now, any scientist would put the wizard's hat on us!

For millennia, astrologers, religions, and people close to nature have been keenly aware of the movement of celestial bodies, especially in the timing of life's matters and in navigation. Mankind simply uses the stars as a giant clock, without a thought for living consciousnesses that might be found within their galaxies. Oh, my Holy Spirit! What do these familiar constellations have to do with living Earth humans?

"Oh, My Linda Layli, Layli Linda! Yes, they do have much to do with some human beings, but not very many, altogether."

Let's play our favorite game! As far as the ability to comprehend these matters, how "old" would you say Earth's population is?

"Linda Layli, since you put it that way, I'd have to say that you, on Earth, haven't even been born yet! There's nothing to build on, in terms of any intelligence living on Earth, able to grasp what We have to say about these matters. That's why such a general question is so hopelessly hard to answer. Maybe, if We concentrate on Ethan, We can speak directly to him, as your conversation had concluded that he and Taylor, are, somehow, connected to the Constellation Orion."

Would it be safe to say that a human drawing such conclusions is probably on target? When my two grandchildren were born, I received specific announcements that they were connected to the Pleiades – as I've been told about myself. Maybe scattered "evidences" are hidden within the minds of living humans, rather than in any other repository on Earth?

"I think that's correct. Transmissions are possible from any higher dimension to any Earthling whose mind can receive them. Telepathy has been around for many generations, and receivers of telepathic information are probably those Starseeds that we have spoken of before in this blog. In fact, thank you so much for reminding Me. This is what the Starseeds are! They're the people of Orion and the Pleiades! And these Starseeds have come, one and all, to elevate the human race by living spiritual lives – though not necessarily within any particular religious designation. Their spirituality may express itself in many different ways."

Let's revisit the question about Freckles, which was dismissed rather cavalierly a few posts back. That writer reported that the freckles on her stomach formed the outline of the Pleiadian Constellation. Any comment?

"We don't think so! We still do not think that anything that distinctive might exist on their bodies."

And yet, the Starseed Eye Syndrome, where the white of the eye shows below the pupil, is connected to that condition! Could it possibly be that, only now, those living in the new millennium time might be showing small clues? I think that we're now floating too far into the unknown, concerning this subject matter. I remember that Your answer to the Starseeds, who have written in, is to "simply relax and leave it alone. Not to try to figure it out." Intellectually, it sounds as if we can't get there from here! Shall we simply conclude that "It is what it is!" and stop belaboring the point?

"Y.E.S! We would be so happy if all Earthlings would do exactly that! Don't worry about this condition! If it exists… Good on you! If it doesn't exist with you… then, good on you, too! This is just too off-planet for present-day Earthlings to worry about!

Focus more on this poor planet, and then, when you die, all will come clear."

A CONVERSATION ABOUT ORION STARSEEDS

In the last post, I wrote of a chance conversation that I had with Ethan Law in Cusco, Peru. He mentioned the fact that he and his girlfriend, Taylor, currently nannying in Italy, share an intense fascination with the Constellation Orion. I believe that he said that the night they met, they mutually admired those stars in the sky over Lake Michigan. Below is a conversation with Taylor, through the comment segment of these blogs.

"Ciao Linda! I'm Taylor, Ethan's girlfriend (though that word never seems good enough). He told me that when he met you, he felt like he was reconnecting with a friend from a past life, so I was really excited when he sent me the link to your blog so I could read about your personal journey and the work that you do daily to help raise the collective consciousness of people on Earth. I want to thank you for this post. I have felt a strong connection to the Constellation Orion for my whole life, even feeling as though it has helped guide me through life in the most beautiful way!

I'm finding that I also connect with and have a profound interest in many other things you have posted about in this blog. What a relief it is to read about other people who have similar concerns and experiences! Thank you for everything you do. Maybe someday I can think of a way to word some of the many universal questions I have, and we will speak again. Best, Taylor

Good Morning, Taylor!
What an exciting turn life is suddenly taking! It's exactly 4:39 a.m., here in the Paz y Luz Meditation Center in Pisac, cradled in the Sacred Valley of Peru. About twenty minutes ago, I woke from a sound sleep when the soft Voice of The Holy Spirit began to speak to me about some of the work I had waiting for me to accomplish on the computer. But, when I got online, I found your comment and realized that I woke up at the very second that you hit the send button!!! The waterfall of significance flows so fast now, I hope I can capture some of it in words here! Plus, sleep sometime, too. Love, Linda

(From Taylor):
Hi again! I really felt the urge to write you this morning, and now it seems like it may have been even more significant than I thought! Yes, I'm currently living in Italy until half July. I can't wait to read your next post! I must admit that I'd never heard of Starseeds until I was reading your blog. I had heard many times of Empaths, Indigo/Diamond Children, etc. But never the term Starseeds. However, it seems like the descriptions I have been reading for the past few days describe me very well, physically, mentally, emotionally, and spiritually. Very often, when people tell me things I haven't necessarily heard before, I get the feeling that I already knew it. Or someone will tell me something of depth that they've learned or realized, even sometimes about themselves, and it feels very obvious to me, as if I've always known it. I'm very open to learning, and I'm never really shocked. I don't know, it seems relevant! I got that feeling when reading the specific blog you mentioned. Hope you're getting some sleep. Talk soon! Love, Taylor

A GENERAL QUESTION ABOUT BEING A STARSEED

Vanessa asks: "Could someone contact me, please? Now that I am looking, I would say that I was born a Starseed, but in the small community I was raised in, was drugged instead of being allowed to evolve. They also did not know that after trauma, many times we need soul retrieval. Please get back to me. I see now that I did have many of the characteristics of a Starseed."

Oh, my Holy Spirit! Would You like to answer Vanessa?

"Y.E.S! I would be glad to. This is a straightforward question, but I wish the answer could be straightforward. I don't think that she realizes just how much We love her.

I am the Holy Spirit and you are not alone, Vanessa. We are watching over you and so are all the other Starseeds watching: those who have already been down there on your planet. You didn't come here to sun yourself on a beach chair. You came to take your chances with Earth as you happened to find it. The people don't owe you anything.

Starseeds have come to change the world by putting up with things! Literally, putting up with whatever you get, in the way of family and hometowns. And then, understanding yourself by taking care of them, lovingly and patiently, so that they can have your example to follow.

That's your mission in life! You needn't stay in your hometown. Don't take Me literally in that respect. However, you mustn't be insulted by someone's rude treatment. Your Starseed designation does not entitle you to any extra respect from the population. But it means that you came here for a reason, or you wouldn't have been given this mission to perform.

So, you are capable of sincerely reflecting back to them love and patience, as Christ did, no matter what is done to you. Don't give people an excuse to laugh at, or persecute you by trying to explain anything, at all, about Starseeds. This designation is only meant for you, and you alone, to know. As your senses open up within your new millennium, then others may publicize their knowledge of their own reality, and you might link up with those who recognize this quality in themselves.

But, don't expect anything from the public. This is not something that was given to you for your own aggrandizement. It wasn't supposed to be bandied about, at all. Starseeds are "seeding" the population so that others will take on higher characteristics by copying your example. Not just occasionally, but as a lifelong practice. It's as if you have known this all your life, and you are sincerely committed to spreading love and harmony.

That's all you need to know about being a Starseed. If this does not already apply to you, in a lifelong, natural way, then you are probably not a Starseed. Physical characteristics are not a dependable sign of this condition. It's your natural tendencies and traits, especially in being known for modesty and an open-hearted love for people and animals, which will confirm your suspicions of Starseed Status.

Basically, a Starseed owes everyone else their own loving understanding and acceptance, while the world does not owe them a thing. But, because these qualities are overwhelmingly attractive, Starseeds usually have many friends and admirers. They are excused from doing anything to live up to this rank, other than being good people. That's what the world needs these days!"

DOES BEING A STARSEED GO AGAINST GOD?

Jill writes: "I noticed the white around my eyes. The white on my left eye goes halfway around and the white on my right eye is like lines between the brown. My ex-husband used to call me Tiger Eyes. I am meeting strange people who are equating some sort of dragon alien with the Pleiades. Some people have merely said that they are 1 of 7 sisters. I'm starting to understand certain things now that people have said this. Why is this so hush-hush? I have met a person whom I have known now for almost six years who has been nothing but horrible to me. But, it seems like I have learned something each time.

I'm confused because I am a Christian woman, and I am not sure if this goes against God. I have had horrific things happen to me, and still survived. Are there people who want to hurt Starseed people? I have also had strange things happen to me since I was a little girl. How do I know, for sure, if I am a Starseed? I also have this freckle constellation on my right arm that looks like the Pleiades and Orion. I am so confused. Please help!"

Oh my Holy Spirit! Jill answered a post about Pleiadian Starseed qualities, and she believes that she might be one. Would You like to first speak to her in general, or to answer her many questions? First of all, let's address her question about whether the Starseed designation goes against God or Christianity.

"No, it does not! In fact, it is in response to the cry of all religions that Earth shall receive help from Heavenly Beings. Starseeds have come from their distant constellations to help the people of these planets where they are born to enter the local population. In doing that, they have become absorbed and hidden deeply within humanity.

They are normal as Earthlings, though they may exhibit some distinctive talents and qualities which they wish to infuse into Earth's future. So, they are legitimate receivers of all of the spiritual teachings brought by every Teacher and Manifestation of God. As spiritual beings, themselves, Starseeds make wonderful Believers, but they are often impatient with the foolishness with which humans have often encrusted their world religions."

Perhaps then, they might find themselves at odds with the established religions, rather than experiencing a feeling that the churches want to close them out? Are Starseeds often the New Agers or the Free Thinkers?

"Yes, and that's part of their reason for coming to this planet: to awaken mankind in many different ways. Jill writes of unhappy times that she has not only survived, but learned from. It sounds like she has been doing her job all along. The good news for Starseeds is that simply by planting themselves deep in the soil as legitimate Earthlings, they have "seeded" the planet.

That's what a seed does! That's all it does! These Starseeds have become rooted people. That was the object. It has already been accomplished for these individuals! Jill does not have to worry about "what she is supposed to do as a Starseed." She has already done it, just by being herself. Osmosis is the mission, and that happened at her birth."

I remember that You once described Earth as a "laboratory" and a "space experiment" where many galactic populations were planted to see how, and if, they could combine. Could they live together in peace? Would they intermarry? Where do our Starseeds fit into that definition?

"Well, really all Earthlings are Starseeds. Usually, when the term is used, you will find it attached to a specific galactic location, simply for Our own scientific purposes. Pretty much everyone is a Starseed, though they may be so ancient that their physical distinguishing marks have disappeared. With the newer ones, some traces may remain.

Those names, Pleiadian or Venusian, don't have much meaning among Earthlings anyway, because none of you have been there to have any idea of those native populations. These are simply Our terms to help Us keep up with our planetary experiment. Basically, the closer that Earth, as a whole, comes to achieving peace, then the more successful this attempt becomes. My advice to all those who identify as Starseeds would be to work towards establishing World Peace!

That way, their own little, individual plant would have "borne fruit," wouldn't it?"

CHAPTER FIVE
THE SOUL AND HUMAN DEATH, BIRTH AND LIFE, ITSELF

WHAT DOES THE TERM "SPIRITUALIZED" REALLY MEAN?

Oh my Holy Spirit! My impression of what You mean concerning spiritualization is more like this: Each one of us is like a light bulb, equipped with certain filaments that have the capacity to generate light and heat. A light bulb can't achieve this potential alone. In fact, if it's never inserted into a proper socket, the bulb will never fulfill its purpose, nor will it contribute any valuable service to the environment. It will simply be a cold piece of glass and metal. Each human must discover their own destiny and may choose whether to illuminate, or not. Spiritualization is simply the act of plugging in and transforming that dark glass into something much more satisfying and useful. To illuminate was within that person's capacity to achieve all along. They simply required the proper energy source. Is that how You see it?

"Absolutely! That is wonderfully described. This is a mystery of life and yet it's still so very simple to understand. Everything is dependent upon light! Darkness prevails and things grow cold without a way for energy to be incorporated into the lives of the creatures. Everyone enjoys modern inventions, including the fabulous light bulb. No one would think of using it for anything other than providing light for beautification and convenience. It would be very foolish to refuse to use light bulbs.

But people think nothing of a refusal to plug themselves into an available energy supply when it's so easy to do that. The reason why churches, synagogues, mosques and temples are associated with the term, spiritualization, is because My Messengers have been advertising this source of Divine Power ever since I began sending Them to advise human beings to plug into Me.

Shall I call Myself *General Electric?* Would that make the concept any more logical and acceptable? How can I make this any clearer?"

WHICH CHAKRA ARE YOU WORKING OUT OF?

Today, I'll tackle the last grown-cold, yellow-pad notes I jotted down many days ago. At the time, I was on a roll with analogies, though I didn't have any immediate need for them. Not wanting to waste a good idea, I captured them sketchily, and this last one actually got a bit of fleshing-out at the time. So here goes:

Let's say that some New Age Analyst gave you a survey sheet to fill out. There's this question about **"Which chakra are you working out of?"** which many people have chosen to leave blank because they don't deal with the modern terminology brought by the gurus, and they have no idea what a chakra is. They don't know about the seven invisible, spinning light vortexes along the human spine, which go from the red root chakra at the tailbone, all the way to the bright white light beaming from the top of the skull. They don't know that people tend to favor one region of their spiritual development, and might even be stuck in a chakra, without knowing it.

Those who operate out of the root chakra lead with their raw emotions and are heavily into the material side of life. Traveling up through the orange and yellow chakras in the abdomen and the solar plexus, one combines the personal, emotional, material outlook with a growing concern for others, until the green heart chakra begins to care more for the general welfare than one's own. The blue throat chakra expresses that concern outwardly through the voice, and the purple third eye of the forehead sees into the spiritual nature of all things. Finally, the brilliant white crown chakra indicates a direct concern with God. So, the question, as to which is your current chakra address, really is an evaluation of where your energy is being directed.

What if our new age census taker has figured out a way to get around this problem of our American, general unfamiliarity with that line of questioning? What if they've couched this in the way of a shopping guide for a fine condominium? Let's see if it would work: Imagine yourself coming to a condo complex, prepared to buy an apartment. You'll be shown around by an agent and, according to your tastes, needs, and budget, you will pick out the one apartment choice that's best suited for you. Here's the tour you'd be taken on:

Basement Studios – These are the least expensive, small, modern, rental efficiencies, which allow pets and are attractive; but have no natural light or windows. These units are very convenient to the outside street, pool, and yard. Nearby liquor store, fast food court, grocery, and subway access puts all city conveniences at your fingertips. However, it's noisy, because of the popular nightclub in that same basement, which operates until the early morning hours. Consequently, there's a fairly rapid turnover of neighbors. The upside is that you'll not be asked to take on any building management responsibilities. They also infer that you can sneak in overnight guests and no one will be the wiser.

Ground Floor –One-Bedroom Rental Apartments – These are larger, plain, modern, window apartments, still very affordable. There's a nice lobby, and even though there's still noise from street, basement nightclub, and entry traffic, it's popular because this is the pool, yard, and cafe level. Pets and one child allowed. There's a rapid turnover and you tend not to know the neighbors very well, but you also have no building co-op responsibilities.

2nd – 10th Floors – Two- and Three-Bedroom Condo Apartments – Family floors, larger and pricier, much nicer, sound-insulated apartments with friendly neighbors, pets okay. There's a Montessori play school at one end of the third floor. A beautiful social lounge and a classy, quiet, fine-dining restaurant are located on the sixth floor. Very little turnover, and these owners are part of the building cooperative with a stake in the ownership and running of the condominium. Therefore, they share some responsibility and are paid a small portion of the building's overall income. They all enjoy large windows and beautiful views with very little outside or inside noise.

11th Floor – Executive Condo Apartments – These are exclusive balcony apartments, each with its own elevator. They are expensive, very elegant and quiet. Pets and children are not allowed, and neighbors are non-intrusive and stable. These residents have a large stake in the building ownership and a very active part in its management, as well as the profit generated.

The Penthouse Apartment – Very large and elegant, surrounded by a lush roof garden with its own pool. Quiet and lovely. Extremely expensive. No neighbors, no children, no pets. Private elevator. The one choosing this apartment has controlling ownership in the building and is the President of the Residents' Association. They carry the overall responsibility for the success of the venture, as well as the lion's share of the rising value of the building. A yacht slip at the nearby marina is included.

So, at the end of your tour, simply fill out your form and select your apartment! Of course, in real life, all of us are constrained by the realities of the pocketbook. But, we also have personal tastes, which tell us what floor we might actually, more completely, enjoy living on. That's the side you must listen to when filling out this form. What lifestyle best speaks to you, right at this moment? That will, very likely, match the chakra that you are now working out of.

WHAT HAPPENS WHEN WE FIGHT DEATH?

My movie of choice last night, set in Denmark, with a few scenes in India, was about a man who was giving away his money because he was dying and arranging his affairs himself, even to bringing in his wife's first love to take over his family for him.

I'd like to ask The Holy Spirit for a comment on the final scene. It was when his body began to go into its last stages, and he became extremely frightened and rebellious about having to die. He cried and cursed and writhed about in the strongest example I've ever seen (not really having had any experience with dying people). I studied that episode with great curiosity, because it certainly epitomized the way many people seem to consider death – and how they refuse to go quietly into that night. But, go they always do, as the next scene of his funeral procession illustrated.

I wondered about the practical effect of all that energetic desire to avoid death, and what it was doing to him, both to his breaking-down body and to his psyche, or spiritual self. Would You give me an overview, Oh my Holy Spirit?

"Yes, I will! Linda Layli, Layli Linda *(He's talking slowly)* has wanted to know about death all her life. I cannot tell you what your own death is going to be like because it will be so different from most people's. You won't have any objections, at all, to coming Up Here – and that's all that death is. Simply an excusing from the hardships of life as it must be lived on Planet Earth. But people don't understand that, and this man was a good example. He had succeeded very much in business and he had a good family with young children. He was only forty-eight years old, wasn't he?"

Yes.

"So, he didn't consider himself finished with his tasks and, indeed, he had been a profligate drinker who probably brought an early death upon himself. But whatever the cause, railing against it will not do anything, at all, to change the outcome. It will only exhaust the person who's trying to stay longer in the world, and they won't be in the same condition as they would have been if they had accepted My Decision to bring them up to Myself at that very time in their life.

You see, it really doesn't matter what age you are when you die and leave this wretched condition of material existence on this terrible plane of living. Things may feel just fine to the one inside of this Earth Life, but it's a very small existence compared to what they'll find on the Other Side. And, the conditions of poverty are not as dire for those left behind as they might imagine. It will be good for those surviving people to struggle, as it has been written for them during their pre-birth planning.

So, don't worry, at all, about anyone else if you should be called, suddenly, to leave this world behind. There's always a condition for your survivors to discover, which will enable them to continue life as they will pursue it, until their turn comes to die. Each one of you plots his or her own course through existence. Many times, I'm right there, near them, waiting to be called upon to help them enter their new condition and overcome any hurdles caused by the death of a loved one.

Anyone who rails and curses Me cannot receive the help that I stand ready to offer. This affects what happens next with them. You asked Me about this dying man's cursing. He will be assisted, anyway, because death is an assisted process. But he, himself, makes it harder for him to accept it. Okay, that's about all I have to say on that subject."

In what way does that angry outburst affect "what happens next" in the dying process?

"Linda Layli wants to know too much about this next stage of life! Suffice it to say that he will be very sorry for this lingering emotion. It's just the same as when you're faced with many kind people, all gathered to greet you and embrace you – and you come noisily, angrily, into the party set up in your honor. You won't feel too good about yourself for doing that! And it takes a little getting over those bad manners among your beloved friends and family members, who are there to greet you after a life on Earth.

If only everybody would just settle into this one, consistently-occurring event in everyone's life. Perhaps, your most important accomplishment, death, is saved for the last minute – and then, you can see what everything meant. And you will understand that your true home lies in these Upper Realms, not down on a paltry little place like Earth. Everything matters; but some things matter more than others. You just have to get out of the Material Realm to realize the truth in "Nothing is permanent! Except life, itself!"

WHAT DOES DEJA VU TELL US ABOUT OUR LIFE?

The Holy Spirit and I have been in touch for hours this morning, and He routed me out of bed right now, to come and write. I wanted to sleep in, but here we are! We have a specific topic to address and that is the question of Déjà Vu – both in general, and also to ask why my friend, Michelle, feels it so very, very frequently. The Holy Spirit's spoken answer was far too complicated to do justice to now in writing so I'll ask again. Okay, my Love, the floor is Yours! What is Déjà Vu, and why does Michelle experience it so often?

"My God, Linda Layli, Layli Linda! We are so happy to have discovered this beautiful spiritual giant, Michelle. Who would have expected to find such a beautifully open individual? Okay, We could praise her for a long time, but she would think that We were nutty and not very organized because We got you out of bed before you wanted to get out of bed; and then, if We just rave on and on and on, you will think that We could have done this without needing to write it down.

Okey-dokey, this is what We wanted to tell you: There is something wonderful coming in the future for Michelle, and We're not exactly sure whether We should explain to her what it is. We don't think We will. Not right now, anyway. Just tell her to expect her life to pick up to an even more interesting level in a few years. She is beautiful, beautiful, beautiful – and We are hoping that she will begin to speak directly to Me. You see, We will be waiting for anyone who's expecting to talk to Someone Up Here, but may not, exactly, be expecting to talk with God or The Great Creative Force. Will she just put aside all of this false modesty and just jump in with two ears?

Let Me say this. I Am speaking to Michelle directly: "I love you so much, and I want to be in touch with you directly – but you might not be prepared for this. Do you know who you are? I don't believe that you have any idea, so just be assured that I love you. I know who you are, and I am here waiting to have a good relationship with you as My Best Friend. Don't worry if this sounds very strange at the moment.

This Inner Prayer Relationship with The Holy Spirit is the most natural relationship in the world, but most Earthlings deny this. They run away from the very idea because they think they must be unworthy, and they suppose that I wouldn't want to have anything to do with them. Well, that's not the truth – but it does result in My being shut out from almost everyone's direct communication. This is a New Millennium! And We are changing many, many things; one of which is, hopefully, the number of people who will want to include Us in their daily lives. So, please talk to Me and I will answer you, and please answer Me and I will talk to you.

Now, about your Déjà Vu. You have been in existence for many, many lifetimes and you have been practicing spiritual beliefs for most of these lifetimes. In one of these lifetimes, you and Linda Brown were sisters, and you listened carefully to what she taught you. Ever since then, you have practiced most of the beliefs that she was teaching you in that lifetime.

Inevitably, you have been instructed by many brilliant lights, and you are meeting them all again in this present millennial lifetime that you are living, right this minute. That's why you keep having these Déjà Vu Moments, because you're very much awake to your spiritual history. The time of your lessons has been concluded, and now you are ready to blossom.

Don't worry. You don't have to do anything at all differently. You don't have to change your plans and drop everything to take up any kind of Cause, just to realize that we can have a friendship. How would you like to be able to pray without doing anything differently? How would you like to meditate, without taking great chunks of time out of your day to get into some uncomfortable position, waiting to hear Me speak formal thoughts into your little brain?

Not to insult your brain! It's not at all little! But, I speak so wonderfully casually to My Loved Ones, and yet, I cannot find very many who will just frolic along through their life with Me, chatting along whenever we find something to talk about. I hope that we can do this, and that you won't put off communion with God until some future time, such as after you retire and grow old and all the interesting stuff isn't happening as much anymore.

I sincerely do want us to be friends right now, and I'm so proud of what you have done with your lifetimes and how you have come into your own! We love you! The Holy Spirit and The Great Creative Force."

7:11 p.m. When I was taking the dictation, I was struck by its sheer "Boyishness!" I even thought that Michelle should read some of my more businesslike interview sessions so she could get to know that side of Them, before I blow her away with this very enthusiastic Lover side.

The Reality of any of these conversations with The Above is usually so very far from what any Earthling ever expects; but this one is a first for me, as well. Would she, could she, see it for what it is? True in every single breath of itself. Or, would she discount it for its complete departure from everything that a human being might be expecting from the Source of Everything That Exists?

No one realizes how badly we creatures have isolated our Godhead. If we ever deign to acknowledge Him, we put Him on some high shelf and act very awkward. He is so hungry for those who will be real with Him; who will not leave Him out of their living moments; who will bounce along, sharing their most intimate and most casual thoughts with Him on a Best Friend basis. The vaster majority of human consciousnesses are so screwed up about His Reality – whether He exists, at all – that for them, He doesn't exist and He's forever closed away from their minds.

A FULL, EFFECTIVE, AND PRACTICAL GUIDE TO COMMUNICATING WITH THE HOLY SPIRIT

Samuel writes: "I need a full, effective and practical guide to communicating with The Holy Spirit."

Oh, my Holy Spirit! Can You give Samuel some instructions as to how a human being can communicate directly with You?

"Yes, I can do that, Linda Layli, Layli Linda. But, it won't satisfy someone who can't even raise his hand in My Direction. Because, do you know what? That's all it takes to start communicating with Me! To simply **want** to talk to Me. Words aren't even necessary. Only a signal aimed at My Name in someone's own mind.

I will answer that gesture. That wish of the heart. And then, the most natural follow-up is the forming of words to establish a two-way conversation.

I think the most difficult part is for the human to listen for My Response in words; or perhaps in a feeling of knowing, all at once, what I want to convey. I can do it in packages of understanding or in specific words. It's then the capability of belief within the human which determines Our ongoing chances of true communication. And this is where the breakdown often occurs.

The listener must believe that they're communicating with The Holy Spirit, or they will not keep trying to engage Me. That's where the problem lies. It sounds too fantastic, and maybe others will discourage that human being from their 'silly claim?' And that's the way that most people drift away from Me – especially if they were children when We began to talk together. Grown-ups don't believe in things like this, do they?

That's also what the religions teach. Most religions tell people: 'Prayer isn't supposed to come with an audible answer. So, don't believe people who say it does!'

Pretty soon, adult humans talk themselves out of simple statements, like:

"Raise your hand and The Holy Spirit will come to you!"
"Speak to Him and He will answer!"
"Ask and ye shall receive!"

ARE SOME BABIES NEW AND ARE OTHERS OLD SOULS?

Tell me about babies. Where have they been before? Are some brand new? Can You tell the difference?

"Yes, We will gladly open the wonderful subject of sending consciousnesses to Earth in the form of new human beings. Some of them have cycled through many times, and are very eager to come back after a long, long wait between lives. Some have never been alive in a physical existence and are coming into a totally different experience than they have ever had before. Many have been asleep, waiting for a chance to descend into an Earth life for thousands and thousands of years, reckoned in Earth time. Without having a moment to think about how they would react, they're born into a totally new environment and have no idea of what they are.

Most are potentially new souls, but at this point they're tiny bits of consciousness. Each has been assigned to a human identity and is setting forth to become a living, breathing human soul. In order to become a soul, each must catch fire with the love of God and ignite that special capacity, latent within. That's the purpose of every person's life cycle on Earth. We can tell the difference between the reincarnating human baby and the brand-new-bit-of-consciousness baby, all the way through their lives. Reincarnating babies are a lot more mature. Their eyes reveal a great deal of depth. The brand-new baby is just a little bit more puzzled and surprised at everything that goes on around it."

When they are in the womb, where are they? Does the consciousness itself reside within the growing embryo/fetus inside of the mother, or does it wait somewhere? Or even hover around the woman who carries it?

"It doesn't have to stay within the developing body cells. Instead, it connects with the growing tissue of its new body, so that it will always maintain contact. But it needn't collapse into such a small area, unless it wishes to. The consciousness remains with the baby, who is within the mother. Frequently, it hovers around the mother, as well."

Does it observe the mother and father and its environment, even before birth?

"Yes, it does. If it's a reincarnating self, it will be able to comprehend a great deal more about what it sees and hears. If it's a brand-new baby, it will begin to take in some of the information needed to acclimate to this plane of existence."

SETTING OUT UPON GOD'S GOOD SEA, ONE MUST FIRST DISCOVER HIS "SOUL LOCKER" AND UNFURL THAT VITAL PIECE OF EQUIPMENT

Here's a bit of dictation I took in December, 2012, in New Zealand. Maybe it touches upon the dichotomy of Body and Soul and how the two can, unintentionally, get in the way of each other. The Body, which is not the part of the Self that comprehends the next world, is frequently the organ we throw into the act of "Getting Right with God." Well, the Body IS the one with which we are most familiar. It also gets us through the complicated act of living.

So we kneel it, and cry it, and sometimes starve it...working so hard to prove to God that we mean business. The trouble is that we're also constantly checking up on this overworked vehicle, looking for signs that it's being heard by Somebody Up There. If we can't feel anything happening, we'll often simply double the effort and try to stave off our creeping doubt.

Meanwhile, our Loves Above may well appreciate the effort and all the signals we're throwing Their way. However, They must wait until this sailor on a foreign sea discovers his own "soul locker" and runs the equipment, which is hidden inside, up the mast. Then, that seaman will find that his soul is tailor-made for this exact type of journey. The only way that the body can help in this endeavor is to get out of the way.

DREAM ADVICE TO POTENTIAL SUICIDES

I had an interesting dream last night, which seems to hold a new attitude about committing suicide. On the one hand, everyone will die sometime, so why not use free will to determine that exit for oneself? One answer could be that it's a mighty messy way to say goodbye to one's family and friends. But, many deaths are messy... right? Typing up my back journals always seems to bring on interesting dreams, and that's what I had done before bed; although suicide was nowhere in them, or on my mind.

However, in sleep, I found myself in a beautiful, tropical, Mexican Riviera setting. Every few minutes though, I had to "reset" myself somehow, in order to tolerate something about this paradise that was rubbing me the wrong way. Maybe I didn't like the food; or the temperature was wrong for me; or I disliked the people; or the noise was too loud. Always something... and I had to sort of shake myself, and thus, turn an inner dial, so that these things didn't bother me.

I realized that this could be an analogy for life. Not everybody likes everything, and we all have to adapt, throughout our course on Earth. Then, the Voice of The Holy Spirit spoke very quietly and clearly. He enunciated deliberately, to make sure that I understood:

"Everyone who commits suicide will be reborn in good, and maybe sometimes in very beautiful, surroundings. But, they will not have the capacity to "reset themselves" in order to tolerate the things that they find annoying or impossible to put up with in their environment. Even in lovely settings, like a beach in Mexico or Hawaii, they will always feel a "little bit off" and they will never be able to reset themselves to feel normal. Also, they will have problems in that life that are the exact opposite to those that drove them to commit suicide. In addition, their body would constantly itch at the site where the bullet, the knife, the rope, or whatever weapon used, might have killed them. In the generalized case of poisoning or drowning, they would tend to itch all over. Their badly-abused body part would always clamor for attention. Paradise has its own unrelenting tortures, too."

Obviously, the core lesson for them during all of this second-time-around life is to take their minds off of themselves. That focus on Self is the core problem for every suicide victim. Another effect would be to provide them with the exact opposite of what they were seeking to accomplish with that suicide. If they killed themselves because of love problems, then they would never find love in this new life. If being overworked was the cause, then they would never find satisfactory work, or even any way to earn a living. If they had turned away from their purpose in that last life, this one would never yield any satisfactory goal.

Usually, the issue of death becomes the unattainable goal in a rapid rebirth. They would have eliminated themselves from something that they already had, and valued. Their messy demonstration would profoundly speak to God about their rejection of what He had given them. Now, they'd forever mourn its loss as their chief desire in a new life, even in wonderful surroundings. People angry over love or family can never have that kind of unity in their next existence. It would be forever out of reach. That's a good suicide prevention argument, for sure!

Most of all, their reset button would be missing. Life would feel "off" to them because they'd done such a terrible act to themselves. Naturally, the solution within this new life of theirs is not to kill themselves once again – and then have to face whatever clever payback might await them as a result. It's also possible that they might have squandered their chances of living any future life at all, because of their rejection. We'd all better make the best of what we've got to work with, right now!

Oh my Holy Spirit! The timing and content of this dream is really uncanny. What is Your comment about those who would commit suicide?

"Dissatisfaction about everything is the "suicide-returnee-to-this-life's" hallmark. That's because they now really have no resources to correct things. They simply have to make the best of what they came out with this time around, because it's their last chance! They have no "Mission," other than to "suck it up" and get on with life... which is exactly what they should have done the last time around. Humans need to get the message that there is no shortcut; but if they want to make it harder on themselves, We can arrange that. However, multiple suicides are simply not going to solve anything."

Do You have any emotional reactions to personal suicides?

"Not really. They do save Us, and the human race, from a whole lot of blither-blather, because they have rejected life itself – and there are plenty of souls waiting and ready to take their place. If they only knew what they were throwing away! So, We don't respect their decision to deprive themselves of a lifetime of opportunity to advance spiritually! If they are lucky, We *might* offer one last opportunity to become spiritualized and send them into a reduced-potential lifetime for a final go-round. If they have rejected their previous actions and wish to still be included within the definition of humankind, they can take their chances with another reincarnation. This will not be an "easy life," though it might seem comfortable. They probably won't be extremely happy, having lost that right to reset, the first time. This is only one definition, out of many, which might become the lot of a suicide. But it fits your dream exactly."

DO YOU HAVE AN EARWIG SINGING IN YOUR HEAD?

Here's a journal entry written almost fourteen-years ago, but still true today. I think many people get songs "stuck inside their head," but they probably never think of this reason. I was composing the words for songs to include in my script, The Candlewick Question, and went to rent some videos in the hopes that they would "set my earwig" to singing.

Let me mention the "earwigs," sometimes called earworms There was a column in the newspaper describing them. They happen when the person hears a jingle, or a catchy song, and can't stop singing it for hours. That independent something in their head, which this newspaper writer named the Earwig, would keep on singing the song to their brain.

I'm well familiar with these inside entities, and they are Whoever, or Whatever, speaks to me on this opened listening channel. They cannot be dismissed so easily as thinking of them as little tape-recorder-singing-bugs. But to someone not attuned to an Upper Presence, this may be the only effect that They can have. The person ignores Them, but sings along with the reflected song. That human would never think of having a conversation with "their earwig," but the so-called Earwig is God, trying to talk to them. It means the person's shield is thin, and they can hear His Voice, but that they don't listen.

You notice that I have pluralized it. I call "Them" earwigs. That's because I've been talking to mine for so long, that the range has expanded, as it will, if you do! You see, the One assigned to Earth as God, The Creator of the Earth, is certainly not alone out there. There are many Beings interested in communicating, once an open channel has been found. My Work is conducted on this opened hearing channel. Nowadays, I'm mostly dealing with The Holy Spirit and The Great Creative Force, and we've finished The Assignment and are in a very casual and easy-going mode. They sing to me a lot, usually all night.

Last night was particularly full of song, a sort of humming, or droning, in my ear. It's often just a way of staying connected and doesn't denote anything of profound importance. Sometimes, it has to do with another person's emotional reaction to me, or maybe, that person is reading my movie scripts, or my letter to the editor, for instance. My Upper Ones tune in on that and report what's going on. If it's significant, They become very loud in Their sing-song. Just this minute, I hear Them as a high-pitched tone in my ears. The right ear, in particular. Now, that I'm mentioning it, the sound has diminished, as if He's listening to what I'm saying, thinking, or writing; instead of letting Himself go on and on.

You see, I must stop what I'm doing and turn my consciousness towards the sound, in order to hear words form – just as you must "listen" to anyone or anything to bring it from background noise into shape as words. In this case, the Inner Earwig sound vibrates along in a fairly fast pattern, until I turn my mind towards it, and focus, Innerly, upon it. Then, it will slow into understandable words.

Before I learned to do this, the Sound would come and go, and would sometimes seem to externalize. I often speak of the years in which I thought that a ceiling light fixture was defective, and then, I'd wonder why so many lights, in so many buildings, had that strange, distinctive, high-pitched hum. For years, I never focused on it – but I heard it everywhere. It was so high and fast because It was frustrated and aggravated that I wouldn't focus to listen. Once in awhile, now, They get that way if there's something exciting going on and, when I listen, I *first hear a conscious slowing down of the sound vibration in order for it to form understandable words.*

Other times, like just this second, I feel a sudden and sharp pain in my eardrum. They're telling me now that it's a way to get my attention; to notify me that They have something to say. At this moment, it's simply to remind me to include mention of the ear-pain signal. At other times, I'll experience a "poof" in one, or both, ears; like an internal change of air pressure. That indicates Their spontaneous, surprise, emotional reaction to whatever I might have thought of, at just that moment. They know my thoughts, because They're listening-in at all times. Usually, it's no surprise to Them, but if I should think of something like: "Last year, at this time, I was..."; or if I make some mental connection, I might surprise Them, and feel Their reaction as a "poof" in my eardrum. Sometimes, it doesn't feel as if my thought was profound enough to warrant that, but it's just a hint about whatever was inspired within Them. I've also mentioned before that I receive many and frequent touches. Tiny pains that come and go. My right knee gets a lot, for some reason. Anyway...my Life With The Earwigs!

IN CHANGING DIMENSIONS BETWEEN LIFE AND DEATH, DO WE ALWAYS RETURN TO THE SAME PLANET?

I'm currently living in Abadiania, Brazil, and taking part in all the activities at the John of God Healing Casa, a very potent place where people come from all over the world for healing and spiritual understanding. I don't need healing but I came to watch. Some of my posada mates learned that I could take dictation From Above and have been providing me with some excellent questions:

Oh my Holy Spirit! Anna, of Florence, Italy, has asked a very deep question concerning Dimensions and places of existence throughout our repeated coursings through life and death. *I know that You were present, listening, while she asked the question and that You understand the true nature of her query, while I might not completely grasp it. I shall try to paraphrase it, though we're working through language difficulties:*

(Step 1) Today, we live in a corporeal body on a material plane. Then we die and leave this dimension to continue to exist "somewhere else," in a place that we imagine to be non-material.

(Step 2) Or, is it merely a different dimension from Earth's, but one that has familiar properties? Possibly, even an appropriate "material form" for that region? Anyway, we know that we continue in our consciousness, and we wear some sort of a body, which feels exactly right to us there. I believe her question concerns:

(Step 3), When we are ready to evolve again into some continuation of our training, within a more restrained existence in a physical body and a forgetful consciousness, are we always limited to Earth, as far as places of life? Or can we hope to move on to higher spiritual dimensions? If so, where might those be? Other planets, perhaps?

"Oh My God, Linda Layli, Layli Linda! What a great, great question! This group of beautiful women is currently bringing life to our writing project! Okay now, let's talk about the subject of dimensional training places. This Earth is only one of many "kajillions" of places of reincarnation in the soul's upward evolution. Earth is very close to the bottom of the pyramid, as you already know, and for that reason, it is serving as a matrix planet – which is a very singular position in the evolution of the perfection of life. Whatever happens here is very basic to what will occur in the Upper Realms. If Our basement is falling apart, it is not a good foundation for the whole of creation.

Many things that began on Earth were giving Us problems in the Higher Realms, because Earth is where We send our young souls to begin their upward journey. Most of them could not graduate from this lower elementary school, because darkness and evil had achieved the upper hand and blotted out the knowledge of God. This blinded these young souls to their own reality as tiny pieces of the One Consciousness, a portion of which was entrusted to them upon their creation. So, these young souls couldn't progress away from this elementary level represented by the simple, three-dimensional Earth."

May I ask if this has always been the case – that Earth was veiled by ungodliness and evil behavior – or has that been a somewhat recent development? Have other Earthly cycles not been so hampered?

"What you don't know is that there have always been consciousnesses capable of pulling out of this swamp, and continuing to higher dimensions after only a few lives. But most people have had to come again and again and again, recycling to lives in a dimension similar to their previous life. Now, however, this new millennium has brought a change in that repeated rotation.

This time period truly fulfills the prophecies concerning The Time of The End! The long testing period is finally over. The examination has produced its fruits and the results are final, as far as this Earth is concerned. Those who didn't qualify for advancement by spiritualizing themselves during their current life on this spiritual-but-physical plane of existence – this three-dimensional Earth level – will be retired, and not sent around to try again in a new lifetime. Their little bit of consciousness will be taken back into The Great Creative Force's Mind, where it originated. They will cease to exist as individuated human consciousnesses upon their death from the current life. If a human has failed to spiritualize, even after many reincarnational attempts, they will go to no dimension, although their former consciousness will exist forever without the distinction of personal selfhood, which had failed to develop itself for so many lifetimes. It will return to its place within the Mind of God.

The golden bits of My Consciousness, who have been able to recognize Me through the murk of materiality and who have spiritualized under these brutal Earthly conditions – those human beings, owners of My Own Consciousness, will go, instantly, upon their death, into a much higher dimension than they have ever known on Earth. It will be both a heavenly and a physical dimension. This is not the same kind of testing field as everyone has experienced during this long, long, long trial to find out "what the *given situation* of this Earthly dimension would produce."

What will happen to this Earth as we know it? Is it evolving upwards too?

"The Earth is in evolution too, because she is also a Being, living in a much larger dimension than any Earth human can comprehend. You, and all of the humans sharing your planet, are simply molecules, or little bacterial colonies, living your brief lives. Recently, you have become extremely bothersome to your host body, the Earth, who is in the middle of her period of testing – and she must bring about her own healing.

There will be a very difficult period while she gets control of the runaway human bacterial population, but the fact that enough of her inhabitants have passed a very, very dangerous and stringent testing period means that Earth has qualified to progress into a higher dimension and will survive to continue to a healthier and much-restored state for her future inhabitants. This will truly be known as a new era of life on Earth, as soon as the dust settles. That may take a little while, however."

Thank You! That was Anna's second question… about a new era, which she senses that we could be entering. She also wondered if the "quality of time" will change, so that past, present, and future will become somewhat the same? How can that be? Or will it be?

"Yes, Anna has perceived a very subtle characteristic of the future of Earth. Life will not be as noticeably segmented, because that's symptomatic of juvenile growth periods. Earth time, in the future, will represent a *coming of age; a Time of Maturity*, when many things will have evened-out. It will be much more peaceful and settled – and there will be such a delightful present that no one will long for the past or dream of the future, but will love and thrive in the present day."

That's exactly what all the Prophecies have extolled, isn't it? I'm so glad to know that we will achieve it!

DEATH AND BUTTERFLIES

Apia, Samoa – As I prepared this book for publication, I included a wonderful story about Sammy, the guardian angel dog, leaping in a field of white butterflies, as seen by his clairvoyant owner after Sammy's death. Here's where I had heard that description before. My Loves Above told me rapturously about the good death that I'll have someday...peaceful and undisturbed. Maybe I'll be alone and separation will be lovely? Then, They described the next moments, and the show-stopper statement was about "Butterflies that would be flying from my hair!" I just HAD to ask about that, because it's an image that, as far as I know, hasn't crept into our Earthly expectations as something that happens after death. It's so "Mary Poppins!"

Oh my Holy Spirit! I'm sorry that I laughed about something that seems to be taken seriously on Your Level, but will You please explain?

"Wellllll, I don't really want to, now; but I can tell you something about it because it doesn't happen to very many people unless they are really, really, really happy individuals who have not let this world get them down, and who see funny things in all sorts of serious situations. You have been doing this all your life, although each episode could have soured you to this planetary life."

Wow! The most recent issue of Newsweek has a cover article, "Heaven Is Real," by Dr. Eben Alexander, a neurosurgeon, whose brain essentially died. He entered a seven-day coma, during which he had incredible spiritual experiences on the Other Side and came back to describe them, knowing full well that his old, scientific assurances were not true. Now, he understood that Consciousness is not dependent upon the cortex! One of the first wonderful things that he reports seeing, during his death, was a beautiful young woman with high cheekbones and deep blue eyes, who flew to meet him across an intricately-colored pattern that he compared to butterfly wings.

I remembered that conversation two nights ago when I took the above dictation. How wonderfully amazing to have such confirmation right away! The Holy Spirit said that people who had endured hard things without letting that get them down – and who could forget or laugh about everything, and be funny and positive people – would not only have these butterflies pour from their heads, but would be followed by them thereafter. Now, more than ever, I want to take dictation about this.

Oh, my Holy Spirit! About the butterflies....

"Oh My Linda Layli, Layli Linda! So much has just happened to change everything, everything, everything! We are not going to tell this story just yet, because it is so uncanny. You have been making these butterflies appear around people's heads for a long time now, after they are kind to you, or become your friend, or your child, or your grandchild. But now that this has happened...this great publicity from the neuroscientist, Dr. Eben Alexander... now things will really start hopping! Anyway, butterflies are going to be more common now that you have clued into them, and We are looking for them all the time, now, too."

Interesting! Because the larva-to-butterfly transformation is sort of a universal symbol of spiritual development and achievement, but it has remained low-key and is owned by no one. Kind of odd, if it truly carries a high status in the Next World. How is it not so well known, Down Here?

"I don't think it is well-known, because, interestingly enough...(*He's speaking thoughtfully, slowly*) "it never used to happen at all, and then it began to be noticed, spontaneously, occurring now and then."

DOES THE PRESENCE OF A SOUL PROVIDE VITAL ENERGY?

This question has to do with points brought up in recent studies pioneered by Michael Newton, PhD, author of Journey of Souls, concerning Life Before Lives. In past-life regression hypnotherapy, he has enabled people to relive their pre-birth planning for their present life. Then, he describes the method that their eternal soul uses to combine with the fetus, destined to serve as its new Earth body. Since this idea was new to me, I asked a series of questions about it. Here's the answer The Holy Spirit gave to the above question about whether the presence of a soul provides an extra energy to a human body:

"Not directly, because that human will survive without the input of the soul during its lifetime, even if the soul is present but masked and denied. Plus, with some artificial-insemination methods of today, when scientists oversee the creation of the embryo, the resulting human may miss out altogether on the combination with a soul, since this addition needs to be coordinated with a Higher Level. That lack can be addressed later, if such a human opens to the spiritual life. So, it's possible for a human to function on a biological level without even missing the inner component of a spiritual soul.

But, there is an *extra* energy available within the soul of the human, which can be accessed by turning in a spiritual direction. This is very observable and I don't think anyone would argue about it, especially if they have recognized their inner soul source and have drawn upon it habitually. Respectfully speaking, the soul is also energized by being a part of a human being's life. It could never function alone in this dimension, so it's absolutely dependent upon a good relationship with its physical counterpart. Together, they function very, very well, with both of them exercising their own free will – but needing the other half to make things work out to the best of everyone's ability.

This is the first marriage that any human faces. Each spouse – the physical brain and the spiritual soul – must learn to co-exist within the temple of its own body. Those who have the most success with this union will have a beautiful chance at making a successful Earthly marriage. Again, here is a pattern in microcosm, which can also be found farther up the ladder in macrocosm. Those with successful marriages have a better chance of creating a harmonious society, and so on and so forth. The simple things become more complex, but at the base, it's all about the marriage of the material and the spiritual."

HEAVEN AND HELL

I was a guest in the home of Tona and Seru, in Suva, Fiji. During a Kava Welcome Ceremony, my host asked this question: Oh My Holy Spirit! Would You please comment on the subject of Heaven and Hell as related in the quotation: "It is the mind that makes a Heaven of Hell and a Hell of Heaven."

"Oh My God! We certainly will! We are overwhelmed in this Kava Ceremony and within the walls of this home. Everything is more wonderful than ever We could have imagined, and very, very deeply spiritual. Everything is even more than We had expected to find on this Earth Below! And We are not just being polite, and We are not just saying this to be a good guest. These are our truly, truly, truly deep impressions. Okay, now We will stop generalizing – and We will specifically speak of these concepts of Heaven and Hell.

These two subjects have been *"beaten to death"* by everyone for centuries in an attempt to warn people about something that is clear to those who accept Me, but is very interestingly confusing to those particles of Myself who simply do not believe in anything higher than the human plane of existence. This is where all of the arguments and embellishments take place.

The believer, who does understand the very simple concept of being reunited with his true self, My Own Self, when he leaves this material plane of existence...this believer tries, through storytelling, to explain to his brother, the non-believer, just how remote he makes himself when he closes off from Me.

I am The Creator of all things. There is no existence outside of My Heaven, because all Being exists within that sphere. But those who deny its existence will remain trapped within their human limitations, even after they have expired and have lost the use of their human body; and therefore they have lost a place in this material plane, which they believe contains all reality. They then cannot recognize Me and their rightful Heavenly surroundings until they admit that I exist.

This is all that Hell is! To be with Me and not to know it!"

THE HALLMARK OF NEGATIVE BEHAVIOR IS ELIMINATION!

Robin, of Rotorua, New Zealand, asks: "Why do our negative thoughts cause disease in our physical bodies? If that's the case, why do we persist in clinging to those toxic thought patterns and permitting such threats to our health?"

Oh my Holy Spirit! Let's consider the whole subject of negative thinking. What could that include? Worry, anger, doom and gloom, chronic unhappiness, sad thoughts, hatred, gossip, uncharitable attitudes, selfishness, ego, jealousy, perversion, incitement of others. Just writing that Dark List creates a certain negative feeling, as my mind searches through the rubbish piles of human behavior for examples. What are Your thoughts about all of that?

"Believe Me, it would be better not to have to go into this at all, because it wasn't supposed to happen this way. I love it that Robin has opened this topic for conversational purposes. It's good to cover the whole subject, in general, before considering the more narrow aspect of the negative thought's effect on the human body. It's very disappointing to Us, Up Here, to acknowledge that the human race is so immature that it can't rise above a certain basement level of looking at this beautiful creation. People's faultfinding destroys natural beauty.

This causes their planet to become exactly what they perceive about it. Human beings do not realize the power of their own attitudes upon Earth's immediate surroundings. All humans are creators – just like the Great Creator is, from Whom they spring! But, they have no mortal idea of what they create with their casually-dropped grousing throughout their lifetimes. They have artistic talent for an exact purpose, which very few realize, even to the extent of unwrapping and putting this glory into practice.

You, Earthlings, are supposed to embroider your matrix globe with beautiful contributions. Instead, some have the audacity to complain about such a basic, unadorned planetary package. A negative thinker is like an artist who hates his canvas because it's blank. Or like a dressmaker who criticizes the dress form, instead of clothing it with original, radiant ways to see the world. I think you get My drift!

HOW DO THE DEAD REACT WHEN HEAVEN IS DIFFERENT FROM THEIR RELIGIOUS EXPECTATIONS?

Susan asks: "Given that nearly all Christian Religions believe in one life with the hopes of entering Heaven, what are the reactions of the people when they cross over into the Realm, which is so different than what they were led to expect?"

Oh, my Holy Spirit! What a very insightful question. I can't wait to see what Your answer is!

"Why not think about the way that all religious followers sincerely feel during their lives, concerning their exclusivity? Every one of them, including the believers within the small tribes, feel that their own approach to God and the Heavenly Realms is the accurate way, and that all others are misguided fools. One of these perfect lessons of life is that they all learn the error of their ways, practically the minute that they leave their Earthly body and resume their celestial identity."

Yes, do go on....

"I Am just thinking about you and your seriousness! You don't see why a religion would teach something so far from the truth. Why should We send these sincere Messengers to Earth, only to have Them form yet another exclusive club, which at its heart, teaches the same Truth that all the others have brought to Earth? They don't seem to stick together very well, do they? I know. It sounds silly to me, too. But, this is the effect that Earth has upon everything that enters this human realm. A general dumbing-down occurs...even within the brains of Our Own Consciousnesses, Our Manifestations of God, Who come to deliver these Truths to the people of the different ages in the life of mankind.

So, this questioner asks an excellent question about the particular reactions of a soul who sincerely followed his religion's teachings, and then learned "at the pearly gates" that Heaven was not so exclusive, or so definitely defined, as they had expected. Nor, were they, themselves, necessarily, who they had believed they were during the life just lived. They might have been a different personality, which might have been hidden from them. There's usually a lot of understanding going on...or catching up to do... and it depends upon how awakened their spirituality had become during that life. Don't forget that some of the most brainwashed of all the religionists are not, at all, spiritually awake – and that's a bottom-line requirement for the kind of instant understanding that's possible to experience upon entering the next plane of existence after death.

If they're closed-minded at death, they will have to undergo some careful counseling before anything will make sense to them. This is one way that life on Earth can set a soul back in its development. On the one hand, it's very praiseworthy that followers have recognized God's Messenger, under whatever name that One has appeared. But, if they behave in an Earthly, possessive manner, having used that religion for adornment rather than enlightenment; then, they have failed one of the hidden tests brought by that Messenger of God. All of life contains such tests – even teachings concerning the end of life. What you are missing here is that:

These teachings are about life on Earth, and they concern your treatment of your fellow man; not about your death and your reward for choosing correctly. Taken altogether, everyone has this same equation. Life is the thing! Not death! As long as you don't fear either one, life or death; and especially, if you don't fear the people sharing life with you, you'll be fine! All humans make their Heaven, right where they live!"

WHY SOME DEPARTED SOULS CAN'T COMMUNICATE

Jessie desires to speak with her beloved grandfather, Pappa, who has passed away. So far, she's been unable to feel his presence or to hear his voice. Are souls sometimes unable, or unavailable, to connect with loved ones? What determines this?

"I don't think I can answer this question specifically. It's really up to each of the participants as to whether they will speak between these dimensions. Partly this is because there are many different places and plans for each soul, once they leave the Earth's environment. Maybe Jessie and Pappa will connect, eventually, but he may have work to do which prevents him from focusing on this planet, and especially upon his dear family members. We haven't ever told the departed not to come to their loved ones, but We advise them to move forward and to advance by leaving the Earth plane completely alone. This is especially important early in their return to the Upper Realms, which are an immaterial place of reality.

The dead don't want to be trapped where matter is more important than it is in the immaterial realms of all possibility. So, tell Jessie that her grandfather gives his greetings, and feels her love for him, and he will *"see her later, alligator!"*

I don't know why you hesitate to write those words. That's what he said to me!"

ABOUT THE FEAR OF DEATH?

It all, ultimately, boils down to the biggie, doesn't it? The Fear of Death? This fear disappears when someone acknowledges a continuation of life on the Other Side, upon leaving the familiar, yet dangerous, physical life. Isn't it strange that the very people who are the most seriously engulfed in the myriad fears generated by this solid, Earthly existence are the most reluctant to leave it behind? They cling so tightly to reality, with its many threats and dangers, simply because they fear that non-existence actually exists! What a conundrum!

"That is the whole thing! *(He's singing in high, excited tones.)* Linda Layli, that's it in a nutshell! If people would only have faith...to the extent of a mustard seed, as Jesus put it... in the everlasting life that continues immediately after they leave their body, then they wouldn't let childish fears cloud their adulthood and keep them from realizing their true potential.

The fear of death is mightily eliminated with spiritualization; but even a rational human can overcome this crippling condition in their life just by relaxing and adopting a wait-and-see attitude, since death is known to be ultimately unavoidable. By all means, do everything you can to stay alive if it is within your power. You can do this much more effectively if you're not dealing with the debilitating effect of fearfulness about your own demise. By all means, becoming cautious about unhealthy habits...and even poisonous snakes... can postpone that final moment of departure, and give you a good life of true adventure

– the birthright of those who are free of fear. But, it won't eliminate death for anybody, at all, at all.

And when I greet each one of you on The Other Side, over here in this very safe place, you will better understand the true reality of these different, but intertwined, dimensions. You will recognize the usefulness of fear as a protection, a training device, and a testing ground, all at the same time. Plus, you will understand how your own elimination of fear, while still occupying a vulnerable body, has enabled a new degree of Heavenly Safety to enter the Earth plane. Your discovery of bravery helps all others to live in greater security."

DO WE ALWAYS REINCARNATE TO THE SAME PLANET

My friend, Pablo, of Montevideo, Uruguay, asks:"I've heard that souls who refuse to advance spiritually are sent to lives on other planets in our galaxy." What can You tell us about that?

"This is the truth and nothing but the truth, so help Me, God! It's much more complicated than the question makes it sound, however. It has to do with Earth's low status among the places of creation in this galaxy and many other galaxies. Traditionally, Earth has been a Hell Realm, and a place of punishment and banishment, where many physical difficulties are encountered in order to force the soul to leave negative behavior behind because the consequences are immediately shown up... in their own bodies and in their surroundings.

To live a true spiritual life here, in this very material environment, is a difficult matter, indeed. It IS a Boot Camp for the soul! Some souls who rise above it do go on to other planets, which are wonderful, higher realms in many galaxies. Some, who reincarnate again on Earth, keep getting themselves into trouble, life after life, and are finally taken off the treadmill as lost causes. They don't go anywhere, as Reincarnation has been discontinued, as of this millennial turn of the Hands of Time.

This is one reason why things are so up in the air, and authority is held in no particular religious hands."

Well, surely, no living being here on Earth has ever experienced the End Times before. Again, Your answer to the question – about beneficial tasks we can perform–seems to fit here, as well:

"Turn, Trust, Try It On!"
And let's add, "Talk to You" –
all the way through this rocky ride!

"Yes! That's all there is to it. It's very simple and very complicated; but just hang on and do your very best! That helps Us, too, and We can form a very good team, which will always help Earth through her own evolution into the higher planes of existence.

Thanks for being aware of Earth's needs, Pablo!"

LIFE IS LIKE THE TOSSING OF GRAINS OF SAND

Journal Notes: April 19, 2004–I had one of those interesting moments early this morning where I came up with a definition, in my sleep, which amounted to utter wisdom. This one was in answer to a testing question given me in my dream – but when this happens, I can never remember what the question is when I wake. Surely, a totally different answer was expected. I know this, because of Their reaction to my strange and unexpected answer. I literally "stopped traffic," and changed the course of things so thoroughly, that the original question was completely erased from the memory of The Questioner. He visualized, so completely, the scene created by my answer, that He admitted He couldn't remember where He was originally going; or what He'd expected me to say. Whatever it might have been wasn't as positive as the idea that I came up with. I believe the stimulus was the sight of a handful of small things, like grains of sand, being tossed into the air. I heard myself giving this answer:

"Life is the time between the split-second that something is tossed into the air and the moment that it lands."

I went on to explain that when it's airborne, it is fluid and can be affected and changed. But, the moment it lands, all becomes fixed and static again. I thought of how a gust of wind could rearrange the airborne particles; or how a chance scattering could occur, due to many causes. A hand might move through them, or a bird, or a vehicle. If the particles themselves had a will to move, then their movement would only be possible during that freedom time, and not before or after the toss-up. This brief life is the malleable period. How are we responding to the opportunities for movement? How do we create our course of events, or react to the unexpected stirrings of our fortune? How do we view the decline –that inevitable second-half of the toss – when we are falling ever closer to the ground? And then, the moment when life ends and the toss-up is completely over? Do we unreasonably wish that the upward ride would continue forever? Do we want perpetual youth and no end to the toss of the dice? No conclusion? No fortune read?

If so, we are foolishly choosing the life-half during which we know very little, and within which we can only discern the blue of the sky. It's simply our exhilaration with the momentum that we're attracted to; not the time of true possibilities after the apex is attained. On the way down, if we should open our eyes and look about, we could see the vast Earth spread below, and begin to draw a few conclusions. Perhaps we would decide to ride the wind and aim for those attractive possibilities we see along the way. Maybe we could soar, instead of plummeting like a rock? Hopefully, however, we'd be good sports about the fact that our momentary ride is coming to a conclusion, when we see the Earth and our own personal landing pad looming ever closer. Who do we think we are, never to come down? Would we really choose to be an "Incomplete Toss?" An "Unconcluded Thing?" "An Unfinished Symphony?" Not I! I *want to do it all, and I want to fully experience that Landing Down. Then, when I'm "Somewhere Else," I'd like to review the toss-up and learn my lessons from it. Yessiree!*

CHAPTER SIX
THE VOICE-HEARING PHENOMENON

HOW MY OWN INNER VOICES STARTED

Thirty-five years ago, a resonant Inner Voice broke into my thoughts:

"Linda Brown! Will you be My Manifestation of God?"

"Yes!" I heard my soul answer!

"Will you eliminate Evil from the face of the Earth?"

"Yes!" Again, this word burst from my inmost being. That sibilant sound was like a white bird released from a cage, darting upwards joyfully and assuredly, as if it knew what this was all about. I still have a stunned, visual picture of that agreement of mine. There must have been some mystic understanding within the bird of my heart, which flew, on a single word uttered twice, up to do her Lover's Bidding.

I, the feet-on-the-ground self, stood dumbstruck at what I'd just witnessed. "What was this? What had I heard? Whose words were those? What had I done?"

I was horrified! I turned away; I refused to listen and blamed my ego for thinking such things – so much so, that no one has heard this confession until just now. Not that I ignored that promise. Day and night, I have worked Innerly to do His Bidding; but three-and-a-half decades later, It's extremely hard to say that Title out loud.

Each human is a universe. We are all profound. But, we're so lonely in our profundities. Every single one of us has that Golden Tether, that Silver Cord, that little nubbin in the noggin of our Creator, from which our own molecule of consciousness was plucked. We all have our own private talking/thinking place in the Mind of God. We can all converse directly.

Not that the shocking question He asked me was broadcast into everybody's thoughts… at that very moment. This isn't mass production! But, what in the world gave me the idea that I was the only one to whom it went? It seemed so personal, that's all.

My object in revealing the following truly-personal information is very innocent. I'd like to compare notes. I hope to open this taboo, "Hearing Voices" conversation. I'd love to make it not so strange to hear the Voice of God...and to answer back in any way you can. We are not as alone as we think we are!

When I began to "Hear Voices," I was asked to choose a Spiritual Name. It could have been anything that I wanted to be called. At first, I was stumped. Much, much later, My Upper Ones realized that I was the embodiment of a Heavenly Super Heroine, called "Innocence." Her complete name was Innocence Gene; and my real birth name is Linda Jeanne, so I could see how that fit. I'm pretty dewy-eyed as far as this world is concerned, so I also had to admit that the nickname was appropriate. Innocence often triumphs in the end...especially over its Anti-Hero, "Guilt." They, in The Upper Kingdoms, have a whole bunch of personified Super Qualities, living down here on Earth, whom They love to keep up with...even to the point of innocent, Heavenly betting. Oh my! Tsk-tsk! Which Super Hero or Heroine do YOU represent?

I'm glad I didn't know that Super Heroine nickname when I made up my alliterative, L-filled, name: Linda Layli, Layli Linda. Here's how that one came about: One day, I was deep in an Upper conversation, when a new Voice joined in: *"Layli? Layli Gundrich? Is that really you?"* Well, it turned out that, indeed, I had been Layli Gundrich, and His good friend, in a previous life. So, when I needed to rename myself, I stitched those two first names together; and not knowing which arrangement I liked best, I kept them both. Quite a mouthful, but it works for all of us.

I put off listening to these inner-sounds-with-meaning for fifteen years, because I was convinced that they sprang from my own ego. Plus, my family was alarmed; psychiatrists had a distinct word for this, which they readily applied; and the spiritual, Inner training that suddenly seemed necessary, simply blew away my organized schedule.

Has this also happened to you, or to someone you know? Well, perhaps it's an ancient subject whose time has come! Too long have the doors of shame been slammed against this mystery! Why should everyone suppose that Voice Hearing is originating in darkness? Here are a few guesses why we've been judged so harshly:

- Popular opinion
- Negative literature and horror stories. Where are the positive role models?
- Religion universally forbids it
- The phenomenon appears uncontrollable
- Fear in the receiver and witnesses
- It comes from an unknown source

Can you think of any other reasons? Science hasn't touched Voice Hearing, as far as I know. Psychiatrists merely label, drug, and long to lobotomize. Mental wards house innocents, as well as those with true diseases.

It's time for veteran Voice Hearers to speak up and let it be known that this ability is really a privilege, if only we'll settle down and get with it. I'll invoke Star Trek and call us "First Contact On Planet Earth," simply for the example I'm hoping to make. Kindly overlook the fact that this curious talent has probably been practiced for millennia. We've all heard of shamans, medicine men, seers, high priests and priestesses. Surely, *something* set them apart from their fellowman, as this reality has done for us.

The difference now is that, with the millennial change, humanity has developed tools to communicate easily – with just a few keystrokes. Conversation has already begun, and a Hearing Voices Network blossoms internationally. In fact, The United States has fewer focal points than other countries do. I hope to change that! It's time we all had a chance to put our heads together and compare notes. I'll go on record right now to hazard guesses about what we might find:

1. Happy, successful, confident Voice Hearers
2. They wouldn't want to be *"cured"* if they could be
3. They have tales to tell
4. They'd love to compare notes
5. About half of them keep it quiet
6. The other half incorporate Voice Hearing into their professions as Psychics, Counselors, Healers, Trainers, Innovators, Authors, Bloggers, Creative People of all identities.

For all, it's become normal and no big deal to carry on Inner communications. For professional reasons, they often downplay this, especially if they've escaped that knee-jerk label: Schizophrenia. It's probably never occurred to most of us to organize a club around this Inner Hearing specialty of ours. But, if we could meet online after someone else has done the organizing... well now, that's quite all right!

The truth that only we, veteran Voice Hearers, can know and prove – with our strong sustainability – is that this is worth it in the long run. We know all about the hardships! We've been in the trenches and have come out the wiser. Perhaps most of our bad experiences could be avoided, once the population calms down? Wouldn't that save a lot of trouble, medical expenses and marriages?

I have tried to include in this book some of my best conversations with The Voice In My Head – speaking to you, the reader, as if you're familiar with the same things. Let's get everything out of the closet and onto the table for conversation! This is not Voodoo, for Heaven's sakes, as you have surely seen! Every personal experience with an Inner Voice, which anyone might ever have had, comes for a distinct reason. As an Inner Hearer, <u>YOU</u> are always in control, unless you abandon that privilege. No problem! You can certainly regain it!

At first, I approached the writing of this *Exposé* about Voice Hearing in the first person singular, as if I'm the only one occupying this brain of mine. But, I've been writing as a team for years – about this very subject –simply not confessing how it felt to have it happening to me. In 2010, I published *"In Secret Diffusion: The Upper Realm Answers Questions About Earth,"* an interview between me and The Holy Spirit, Whom I settled upon as the One who must be speaking to me, because He was such a high Good Guy. I made up a long list of cosmic questions and transcribed His excellent answers. Soon, our website, www.insecretdiffusion.com, solicited more cosmic questions from the public for my blog. Throughout this book are samples of those questions from the public. You are welcome to submit your own general and vast questions to www.insecretdiffusion.com. I've become the Ann Landers of the Spiritual or Cosmic Question genre.

MY CO-AUTHOR, THE HOLY SPIRIT

Oh, my Holy Spirit! Since You are the main Voice in my head, would You like to say a few words on the subject?

"Yes, I would be happy to, Linda Layli, Layli Linda. You and I know who we are to each other – and that says it all. Probably, this is true of all Voice Hearers concerning the personality Who speaks to them. We, too, need to address each other by name to have any real, long-term relationship. So, My first advice to a new Hearer is to get friendly with your Good Guys, and your Bad Guys, in there within your head. None of them can hurt you, at all. Some of them might be trying to confuse you for their own ends, but there are always Good Guys overseeing this process."

So, the name isn't for bragging rights; it's just the best one to define the Being. It, somehow, "feels right" to the human who gets into this strange position in the first place. Tell me, why do we get chosen to be spoken to?

"This is a delicate subject, I don't mind telling you. Everyone who hears Voices in this 'Manifestationship Millennium' has shown the capacity to look within themselves and to turn upward to the source of their own consciousness. They have been groping, for some time now, for God; and, at last, He can contact them directly. This is a huge change in the way things were run in the past between The Creator and The Created.

We are proud of the Hearing Voices Network and this new attempt to explain everything to the public. The use of the brain in this way isn't supposed to be scary or dangerous, nor is the learning of things directly from your Upper Characters intended to be frightening. They've always been watching over the people of this planet. You do describe it pretty well. This is a new day for humankind!"

It's not always fun and games for the person whose Inner Hearing Channels suddenly blow open. Will You please comment on this?

"Yes, it's often the most difficult test a human can ever have, unless they're born with their Inner Hearing Channels open. Then, parents will often try to train the child out of seeing or hearing things like their imaginary friends. Even so, these people often don't detach, but go underground, as do many who struggle with this basically incompatible proposal: that they're being contacted by invisible entities. We will also discuss briefly the small band of negative spirits that still plague these innocent and unprepared opening souls. They are actually fairly easy to deal with, once someone knows what's going on."

That's where the interesting "battle tales" will be, along with any unfortunate consequences that alarmed family members might bestow. I'd like to ask about the mechanics of all this. How do You physically connect with our brain tissue? Or, is it only the pressure of the sound waves produced by Your Voice that I feel inside my head?

"This is also difficult to convey. Only certain people can take this vibration, but that's what sound is. It has to connect with auditory nerves and create pressure on the eardrum in order for these thoughts to create impressions within your brain cells in the form of inner sound. We do communicate differently with different people. Some don't feel pressure on their eardrums or brain tissues, which are very sensitive to incoming messages. This sensitivity is why things sound very noisy sometimes. Also, that can be affected by the excitement level of the hidden Speaker, Who may tend to talk much louder than necessary."

Oh my Holy Spirit, when a baby is born on Earth, what's the state of their spiritual inner hearing channels? Or, is there really any such thing before they develop that during a lifetime?

"Linda, this is the whole thing. It's not something that humans are generally equipped with. Not something that was planned for physical life. Quite naturally, Those in higher planes of existence, places you would consider non-physical, have means of communicating with the Realms Above, as well as with each other."

Telepathic?

"Y.E.S! Brain cell to brain cell. Something similar to this takes place within your own body, in organizing itself, but on a microscopic level. However, that doesn't usually interfere with someone's intellectual thoughts because they need their attention turned to the matter of living in an external condition. The same goes for their place in the cosmos. We don't want to create information overload."

So, what causes these Inner Channels to come online?

"Well, that's actually up to the organism itself. Sometimes, it returns to birth in a new life with a well-established habit of communication with its Source, and thinks nothing of this back-and-forth contact. Often, this depends upon mankind as a whole. When a planet's population elevates within a Harmonic Convergence, as has happened with the turning of this Millennium; then veils are stripped away and many human facilities are suddenly expanded. This can be quite surprising until the phenomenon becomes more familiar and normal to the human race."

Do more people now "Hear Voices" than in the past, or is it simply easier to share this startling information now?

"Well, We've always talked to some humans, so We won't hazard any guesses. Let's just hope that the human race will take advantage of these information opportunities. There's still much to improve, beginning with humanity's propensity to slaughter itself. Let's give Peace a chance! Then, watch out for more of these strange qualities to elevate the spiritual vibrations of the planet."

Just a few decades ago, the phenomenon of Near Death Experiences broke into public knowledge and gave us an inside look at the beautiful sequence of a transition out of a life on Earth. This helped reduce the fear of death, and created an appetite for more and more of those personal NDE stories. I see a similarity between that glimpse of the Next Plane and the Hearing Voices phenomenon – especially because it removes the stigma of mental health issues that many have had to bear. Do You have any comments about these similar insights that have been given to us?

"You're in some kind of classroom now, as a human race. These are your lessons. Some of you will learn and some will not. Teaching is always more effective when delivered in the form of personal stories. Keep being interested in these beautiful examples, and they will teach you much about the Next Worlds and your place within them. Earth isn't the only place of existence, and that should be a comforting thought."

Many people are simply afraid of this subject of communicating with Invisible Beings. It can sometimes feel quite negative and aggressive. Why is that?

"Well, there are also mentalities who have died from the physical plane, but have not risen above the Earth level in their consciousness. So, they have no place to go when they die. Their focus is downward, and usually tied to some addiction. They want a human body to occupy for as long as they can commandeer it. Open hearing channels give them a chance to grab hold and scare a poor Earthling into doing their bidding. A strong living personality, connected to a Higher Plane, won't put up with this annoying interference; but if fear enters the equation, then that human becomes weakened and possibly victimized. All they need to do is to take control. That's a learning curve, right there!"

So, becoming pestered with angry energies isn't Voodoo or evil! It could simply be a desperate, ghostly hitchhiker. What's the solution? How does one take control?

There's nothing to worry about! You can actually help this lost personality move on, simply by referring them to their Creator through your friendly conversation with them. That may be all it takes to separate them from the lower levels. Just don't worry about it. This is how you gain your own experience – and your skills in communication and discernment – when you don't have the usual, physical tools. It all comes out well with practice, and you'll leave that noisy, Earthbound level behind as your living consciousness matures and rises to the higher levels."

Do You mean that we can remain alive and in touch, Upperly; but will not relate to this Spirit Band close to the Earth's atmosphere?

"Yes. That level, or stratum, also contains negative vibrations caused by acts and emotions of the living. It still affects this planet; but, hopefully, it will disperse in time – especially if each of you will do your bit when given the chance. These are the difficult energies that become audible to the humans who have open hearing channels. But, they only temporarily impinge – usually while one is getting used to the presence of a new auditory source."

WHO is this speaking to us in our heads? One or many? Some people call their Invisible Speaker by a certain name. Others say it is "their own self." Or, maybe a relative? A historical figure? Who? God? Angelic Beings? Saints?

"There's no particular pattern. It can be many Sources, and each of you finds your way to the best one for yourself. It all works out wonderfully! My advice is to simply trust in your Source of Information and learn whatever you can. We are always trying to awaken a potential Hearer, and We will speak in many variations."

So, these are our Invisible Friends – now coming to adults, as well as to children?

"That's right! It's a new day, and We have new ideas to deliver. It's okay to be innocent and childlike again. Just consider these Voices as friendly companions and teachers, and enjoy Their enriching company in your life."

MY FIRST MEMORY OF SPEAKING TO THE AIR

"I am an Idealist – and somewhere in the world is a Cause that will take me around the world!"

It must have been around 1955. I was a teenager, maybe seventeen, standing in the upstairs bedroom that I shared with my sister, Ann. I was alone. Suddenly, for no apparent reason, I turned to the left, somewhat facing the side window, and I raised my hands in a gesture of open acceptance and willingness. I began to speak aloud to no one... to the air...to, simply, the window... and that is what I said!

"I am an Idealist – and somewhere in the world is a Cause that will take me around the world!"

I'd had no experience of speaking to the air. I had heard no question, audibly or within my head. I didn't wonder about that statement, nor why I said it. Plus, I have remembered it over all these years, perhaps sixty, and I'm a famously good forgetter. I wasn't a traveler at the time, and I didn't even have a strong desire to see the world. My statement came out of the blue. And then, it sat there in my unquestioning consciousness. And, that was simply that! Genetically, I have sea captains on both sides of my family. Was this my heritage revealing itself? Late in life, I've done as much, or maybe even more, world traveling than my ancestors might have done.

I *was* an Idealist, but not religious, in spite of the fact that my family and I attended church every Sunday. I believed it all, but was bored with Christianity's repetition and total lack of originality. However, I really cared about what God thought of me. My girlhood was straightforward and boring. A bit like church, I suppose. Just mild and simple in Winter Haven, Florida.

But, here I was, announcing idealism and the idea of traveling around the world??? We were poor... well, genteel poverty, anyway... having an absentee father, who by that time had not only been away at sea for years at a time, but who had actually divorced my poor, shy, overwhelmed mother, with four girls to raise; leaving us plopped at her mother's home to get along as best we could. It was hand-me-downs and no spending money. My father married someone else.

I have no idea how we afforded ourselves, but we didn't have any sort of poverty mindset. My sister and I did well in school: she, in scholastics, and I, in student leadership. The big house was the one Mother grew up in. I knew nothing about where the money came from, nor thought anything about it... but here I was, upstairs in that bedroom, announcing such Grand Plans to myself... and to the air! After that one brief, dramatic moment, I simply went back to putting on my makeup, or whatever I'd been doing in front of that old vanity. I never questioned my odd statement. Atypically, I never forgot it!

I'm now metaphysical! I hear Voices! I'm Clairaudient! Long ago, when the Voices first started – at age forty-two – I remember "seeing" things, as well. Perhaps I was developing Clairvoyant skills, too? Both were brand-new to me – and both represented an alarming development to my family. My physician husband and two teenagers did not welcome craziness in their stay-at-home Mom. No way, Jose! Scary stuff!

I'd always been a sensible, feet-on-the-ground, happy-go-lucky good leader and savvy person. Not someone being spoken to by Invisible Forces, Sources, or Friends. Certainly not someone being trained by Inner Presences to fall into random trances and stop paying attention to household duties, for heaven's sakes! This was not cool! It must stop! Right now! At some point, I remember standing in front of another window somewhere in my house and saying to the Air:

"I wish to have Insight in plenty; but please excuse me from having Inner Sight!"

Kaboom! Just like that, the Vision-ability shut off. It went to black – and I haven't seen those entrancing pictures since. But, I've had massive evidence, over the years that followed, to prove that my Insight has become better and better. Just because of the brief time I did perceive those Visions from the Other World, I knew that place to be really amazing. So pretty, I couldn't stop watching! They always caused me to go into trance. Therefore, I needed them to discontinue, because I couldn't relate to the real world while that was going on. Little did my teenage children know what I sacrificed – just to be there, mentally – when they came home from school! To this day, I can't "see" anything in there when I close my eyes and even just try to visualize something. I do imagine, in some way, but when a meditation leader narrates a scene and then asks me *"What do you see? What does the book page in your hand say?"*– I haven't a clue.

Even without vision, my Voices continued attracting my consciousness to Them. They might come to me, day and night; awakening me to another reality through sound, if not through vision. I knew that They were good! I knew that They were God! The main one finally settled out to be named The Holy Spirit.

"All is well! Just talk to Us. We have things to teach you!"

It wasn't long before I had my real-world showdown! One midnight, my husband demanded to know what was wrong with me. I faced him squarely and said that I was "Hearing Voices!" Although I didn't want to, in the least, I also obeyed the command from Within to announce, loudly, to him, three times: "I am The Manifestation of God!" Good and all-knowing doctor that he was, he grabbed my long, auburn hair and, using it as a leash, pulled me out the front door. The hair-pulling caused me to bend over forward to follow him. How strange that is to describe now, but it's the ignominious way that it happened. He led me, barefoot in my nightgown, four blocks through our lovely neighborhood, to the emergency room of the hospital, where he was a staff physician. I was admitted in the dark of the night.

During my two weeks as a patient, all the Psychiatrists agreed that *"If she's Hearing Voices, then she surely is wacko! Schizophrenic! And she needs drugs for the rest of her life, simply to stay sane and acceptable to society!"* During this enforced vacation from real life, I befriended other patients, some of whom had the same symptoms as mine. "Someone" was talking to them from inside of their heads. They were as surprised and as confused as I was.

At first, I refused the medicine, but I finally accepted it, and the Voices left me alone. Apparently, we "taste bad" to Them with drugs in our system. They'll never mess with your mind when you take that stuff! Yuck! It dries up your saliva and makes your tongue stick to the roof of your mouth. You can't think clearly, and you become a true dullard. And THIS is the way that they get you well? You may not hear or see things – but you don't function, either! Society has its ways to make one conform – and this is the stupid state of medical science, even in this day and age. Destroy the selfhood, the verve, the originality, the smile, the life within; but leave dull emptiness to behave itself, when we're way too old to play with our invisible friends.

Naturally, my behavior soon returned to "normal," though I was a little loopy from the meds. Another taste I experienced, of the (literally) "dopey" medical world my husband so relied upon, was my post-release visit to Dr. H, my psychiatrist, for counseling sessions. He couldn't have cared less about me! Usually, doctors' families get the best care of all, but that didn't happen in my case. I'd hardly seen Dr. H. in the hospital, and there were no soul-baring sessions attempted, to discover what in the world was going on inside of my head. Clearly, he felt that we were all crazy, up there, in the psych ward. End of story! No sense in going into detail to make us spill our beans. We wouldn't make any sense, even to ourselves, and that was just that! Why waste the doctor's precious time?

However, after release, there was a mandatory need to sit and talk before his desk – for, say, half-an-hour – before he could scribble out another prescription for the drugs, which I never took anyway, once released. These were pills, they said, that I'd have to take until I died. Or I'd flip out again. Well, I prefer the "flipped" state to the zombie state!

Most insulting was the boredom with which the doctor pretended to listen to me. I even caught him falling asleep when I was sincerely attempting to explain what I didn't understand myself. He, clearly, wasn't into the spiritual/metaphysical aspects of life – especially if they didn't jibe with his own belief system. We were just the "Crazies," lost in our twisted view of things, who had nothing of value to say. His only sign of life was when he roused to tell me that my time was up and to hand me a prescription for more mind-numbing pills. Quite possibly, these were the psychiatric drugs that others kill for – but not at all desired by me.

Another physician, just as jaded, simply delivered the word "Schizophrenia!" when I asked what he thought was going on. To me, this exposes the total inadequacy of Psychiatry in 1980, but it probably still represents the practices of today. Maybe others, less trained, will hear you out as Counselors; but these Gods in White Jackets don't care in the least. Ironically, my state of health, today, is so robust that I need no medications or treatments, at all, for anything. I'll bet that I've either outlived, or am healthier than, all of those who tried to deliver their vaunted chemical cure on me, thirty-five years ago.

Anyway, I went back to my family with this terminal diagnosis. "Terminally Nuts," that is! Not even the slight dignity of Religious Fanatic; which I'd have hated, but recognized as ballpark, none the less. I didn't want to be goofy. Wishing only to raise my kids and be a good Mom, I went out and bought a Sony Walkman, in the day when cassette tapes went into a little player around your waist, attached to headphones. I turned mine up, real loud, so I wouldn't hear any more Voices in my head. Opting out of that mysterious spiritual education, I took many long walks with that contraption on.

Voila! The tape player would suddenly break! *"What's this? Water in the heads inside the machine? How could it get in there?"* The thing was broken and I'd go out and buy another one. Not cheap! Soon, the new one broke and I'd find wet tape heads again. Five Walkman units broke in a row during the time I was struggling to regain control of my own life, hoping to become sane like everyone else. At last, the Voices abandoned me and I was free! I went back to normal life. Helped my son select a college; grocery shopped; walked the dog; vegged out like everybody else; watched TV after dinner. Everyone but me was happy about that development.

Years passed! My kids grew up. I left my husband and could do whatever I wanted with my life. I moved to Aspen, Colorado; learned to snow ski; worked in retail; moved to Atlanta for four years to plan and lead peacekeeping tours to the Soviet Union. Thus began my lifelong habit of world travel.

In the early 1990s, my elderly mother became ill, so I left international travel to become her caretaker. Kaboom! My Voices returned, loud and clear, after fifteen years of silence. They hadn't gone anywhere! They had just waited quietly in the background. Later, I learned that I'd become a virtual TV star for the Upper Regions. They had needed an Earthling to follow around, in a quest to find a "good woman" on the planet to represent the human situation here. I'd answered affirmatively to that loud question, initially posed to me, about being God's Manifestation. That gave them permission to do what They liked with my life and my head. For fifteen years, during the silent period, I had no idea that my boring activities and ordinary words had been studied as a representative sample of Earth Life. The viewing screen was the inside of Their eyelids, when They shut Their eyes. They watched me, this "little Earth woman, doing her honest little life." I didn't know any of this, of course. Now, there's where any Psychiatrist would say "I told you so!"

and any man of the street would concur. You're probably thinking that right now, too. I'd surely have agreed, if I'd known this then. It still sounds crazy!

Points like this are what I write about in my journals, and those have been buried in family storage places for years... all these years.... not even collected very carefully into one group; and not many re-read by me. Simply slightly remembered. These secret journals are the ones that I've now been instructed by my Author Within... to reveal to the world with this book. What? I'm to publish my private stuff? But, I don't *want* to! I really don't want anybody to know about it. Why should I confess to this Inner Eyelid story? It sounds nuts to me, as does so much else about this whole subject. The only thing is that now I can prove I'm not crazy. I've lived alone, very successfully, all these years; I've written almost five-hundred blog posts; published four books; traveled the world, alone, for so many, many years. I couldn't do that if I were crazy, could I? No. I've outlived that diagnosis!

Writing has always been important to me. Perhaps it's the reason for my sanity? To massage my life and all of its unique happenings – and now to publish even this much – has fulfilled a youthful wish of mine. I remember wanting to speak to a star by tossing words aloft and letting them float on currents to the ears of others, unknown to me. When asked to explain why I'm an author, here's what I once wrote:

"The letter I held in my hand was one-hundred-years-old and very delicate. Its pages were thin and closely-written on both sides, with now-faded ink. The handwriting was flourishing in the British style of elaborate penmanship. As if that weren't barrier enough, the pages looked like plaid! My long-dead great-grandfather, Henry Hilgrove Hollis, merchant captain of The Harvest Queen, out of Bailey's Bay, Bermuda, employed a common technique to use his postage well. After covering all surfaces with his cultured script, he turned the pages sideways and layered more evenly-spaced thoughts above the first...crosswise. Now and then, a third layer went on, cattycorner. But, usually only as a postscript. Henry's letters told of life aboard a three-masted, wooden Schooner, sailing throughout the West Indies and much of the world.

His young wife, Louisa Jane Wilkinson Hollis, tending their babies back home, would reply in similar fashion, but with a more feminine writing style. Her letters told of daily life in the mid-1800s, with news and gossip about family and friends. Candid windows into a time gone by.

We had them all, Mother and I! These were her Bermudian grandparents' love letters. Seven- hundred fat envelopes of precious correspondence, sorted into chronological order. It was our daunting task to transform them into readable shape. Of course, they were written in English, but their cross-writing had kept them secret from any prying eyes. Not that there had been any curious intruders in Mother's attic all those years. Now, in retirement, she set about transcribing the historical letter collection into her own, much more readable, longhand. I typed up her work: first using my clunky, manual typewriter; and then, a modern electric one, throughout the '70s and '80s. When we finished that ambitious project, I took the letter collection and our readable translation to Bermuda and presented it to the Bermuda Archives.

Blessed, loving words between a man and a woman. A husband and wife, separated by the sea during most of the fifty years of their marriage. Such precious, long-awaited missives were the very sinews of their life together. Through these, they raised their children, stayed active in their local friendships, and most of all, declared their evergreen love for each other. The written words of these unwitting histories introduced me to my youthful antecedents, and I became acquainted with them as newlyweds. I still recognized them in old age, when Henry finally left the sea and stayed at home. Then, they wrote to grown and married children: my Florida-bound grandmother, for instance. Louisa saved every letter she ever received, bound in ribbons in her cedar chest.

Irrationally, I wished that these long-dead great-grandparents of mine had addressed even one word to me! I wanted to feel a love like that enfolding me, too. That's when I coined the phrase, "Speaking to a Star!" signifying remoteness...in time, in place, in tongue. Sent out, as if from a ship at sea in a foreign port, to wend its feeble way to me – so far ahead in future time, but on the way to life, nonetheless. Though I should take one-hundred years to materialize, my courageous, lonely captain would simply have to believe that I would someday feel his love – and send it on to me.

That set into motion the idea that I, too, could "Speak to a Star," as well. That my own written word might survive, as Louisa's and Henry's had, to reach someone, now unborn – and to teach them what is in my heart. That fragile letter in my hand was proof that it can happen... even without intent. As an author, I vowed to add intent! Not only for survival, but so that my message would steer its way through the course of time, destined for related, waiting hearts.

I made that formative Speaking to a Star decision in my thirties. Letters could not be the avenue I used, having no recipient to send them to. So, I chose an even more effective route. A journal! These bestow much more privacy than correspondence, and I employed them well, as my burgeoning spirituality went through its gyrations. Personal crises in my newborn's health; clashing opinions in my marriage; ponderings on life in general – all took refuge in those waiting receptacles in ways that only personal journals can fulfill.

I can't begin to guess where all those records are. Boxes. Storage sheds. Daughter's attic? Forty years' worth of composition books, during which my intimate and very unique conversations with Voices In My Head became a factor. Two-way, written conversations. What a treasure! I wish I had them all to read again. Some, I have copied out on my hard-drive, so I know how good it gets. But all except the six hand-written notebooks, dragging along with me in my travels these days, are simply "somewhere else," as out of my control as Louisa's letters are to her.

I've certainly achieved my first objective: to capture down my thoughts as they occurred! I've taught myself to write by practicing the art for all those years. I've forgotten what I said at the time of writing, so that I'm the most pleased of all the readers, if I should stumble upon them once again. And I've set my little paper sailboats out upon their incredible journey across the Sea of Time. May they find their waiting Star – most likely, yet unborn – who treasures them enough to set a pen in motion and record their own stuff of life.

HOW MY LIFE DEVELOPED AS A SILENT PSYCHIC

I wasn't at all psychic for the first half of my life. My culture was ordinary Floridian, Southern, Episcopalian. Nobody referenced anything "spooky," or inward. In adulthood, my sister and her husband joined the Church of Metaphysical Christianity and my mother followed suit, but I wasn't interested.

Then, I became a member of the Baha'i Faith soon after my first child was born, and that Faith taught not to mess with anything psychic. I was a devoted Baha'i for thirty-three years and expected to remain so forever. This wonderful world faith invites all people and religions to unite under its banner, because it fulfills the prophecies and promises of Earth's former Revelators. According to its scriptures, the Baha'i Faith was destined to become the one world religion as the people of the planet realized their oneness under its banner. For three decades, I used my organizational skills to serve this exciting new peace-loving religion, and, for awhile, I even produced weekly radio interview programs run on several Central Florida radio stations.

"Martyr me! Let me give my life in Thy Service!" was my constant prayer. *"Test me, oh my God! I wish to give my life's blood for Thee!"* I prayed a lot in those days, and I began to serve in larger and larger capacities – especially by helping to organize group trips into the Soviet Union, full-time for four years, between 1990-1994.This devotion to the Baha'i Faith and its outward effect on my life was in full swing.

Suddenly, my contact with an "Inner Voice of God" popped up in 1980, and I was considered well and truly crazy by family and friends. I'd never gone into trance before, nor had I heard of Voice Hearing happening to ordinary people. I did whatever I could to stop it. At last, I prevailed in my inner request to lead a sane life, and to stop hearing those disturbing sounds in my brain–and the sound stopped.

WHAT DOES IT FEEL LIKE AND WHAT ARE THE RISKS?

Inner vocal sensations coming from an unknown source, not your own mind, actually do pulsate inside of your head and bang upon your inner ears. This can be very, very persistent! Often, the Voice is a good and comforting one, and I could easily accept that It was The Holy Spirit, as It had announced Itself to me.

But, I also became familiar with a Negative Level, which I began to call the Green Goblins. Apparently, the invisible realms around Earth contain unspiritualized departed beings, which can become pesky to anyone with newly-opened hearing channels. This fact alone presents a very good reason why we need inner training in a new spiritual talent just as soon as it begins. Otherwise, we can become sitting ducks to ghosts wanting to return to Earth any way that they can. I had to learn how to deal with those entities, and to tell the difference between the Voices of The Holy Ones and any departed humans with nowhere to go after death, who were seeking to invade unwitting channels for a temporary return to Earth. It's not that hard to protect against this auditory invasion, once we become trained. That's why I kept going into trance just as soon as I could hear sounds in my head.

Anyway, back to the Baha'i Faith. I'd begged off of Voice Hearing for fifteen years, and had, pretty much, forgotten about "whatever that was" that had interrupted my life so long ago. I was proceeding with my Baha'i life: divorced; kids raised; working in Aspen, Colorado, and learning to snow ski, mid-life. Then, in 1990, I moved to Atlanta, Georgia, to work with the newly-emerging field of Citizen Diplomacy to the USSR, helping to bring peace between our almost-warring countries. What a glorious and adventurous time that was! I was writing large upon the world! And I didn't hear the Voices to interfere with my happy, travel-filled life.

Three years later, my mother needed me to care for her in Winter Haven, Florida. At eighty-seven, she was simply too weak to live alone, but she was still healthy and had a good and lively mind. For years, she had devoted herself to our family genealogical project, organizing and transcribing the love letters – written by her Bermudian grandparents – which I'd always helped her with. We again took up that task with great gusto and, with the help of my sister to cover Mother's needs, I was even able to plan and lead one more Soviet trip to Siberia, working from Florida on my new DOS computer. Our group went to the Lake Baikal region of Russia, just above Mongolia, the furthest that I had traveled thus far.

Sometime late in that three-year period of Mother's care, the Upper Voice broke through to me again, and I heard the very same question that I'd originally been asked by that unmistakable Voice, way back in 1980: *"Linda Brown! Will you be My Manifestation of God?"* As before, I witnessed my own Inner Self answer, instantly: *"Yes!"* The mission was the same simple request: *"Will you eliminate evil upon the Earth?"* And, as before, *"Yes!"* flew out of my inner throat. It was my soul, answering His Call… the very same Call I had received in 1980.

"Oh my gosh! It's real! This was really real, after all! I wasn't making this up!"

Part of my shutting down and putting on the Sony Walkman headsets had not really been a worry about craziness, but a horror at myself about the very idea of such an overweening presumption of my own ego. To think that I might have heard those profound words – and that most unusual request – whispered into my brain! And then, to have heard such an audacious response coming from my own throat within a place down deep inside of me! Just ego? Twice? The relief to know that I hadn't made it up, that my own ego hadn't manufactured it to fill some psychological need within, was immense! *"I'm going with this! I will trust what I've just heard! Yes!"* was all I needed to say in that instant.

I told no one!

Again, I had to be silently trained. Would I obey in a heartbeat? Would I trust Them, and do exactly as I was told? Could I even hear Their Commands? Could I (and more importantly, would I?) carry out the sometimes outrageous things I was ordered to do during this training period? Well, almost not!

One test was so odd that it could have had me arrested. But, I did it! I was told, at dawn, to run from our porch, naked, to the intersection at the corner – practically next to the house – and stand facing east, raising my hands to the sky for just a moment. Then, I could run back inside. What? That took a lot of moxie, but I did it – all the while being super-conscious of the home across the street, which contained a large and lovely Vietnamese family. I imagined every eye trained upon me. But, I'll never know if there were watchers. They didn't turn me in.

Another episode was a command to lie in bed at the hour I should have gotten up to go to my job as an Adult Education teacher. Mother called up the stairs when I didn't appear; then, she struggled up to see why I hadn't responded. My Holy Ones instructed me not to move a muscle, but to pretend to sleep. And so I did, though it went against my every grain.

Mother called 911 and I was moved into an ambulance, which had backed up to that very same front porch door that I'd recently run naked from.

Once inside the ambulance, with a male attendant sitting beside my head, I was commanded to announce, in the loudest possible voice: *"I am the Manifestation of God for this day!"* three times. "Oh no, not again!" said I to myself, but, I did so, and I was shocked to feel the body of the ambulance shake a bit from side to side. Of course, it was also starting to drive across the lawn. Surely, that attendant had a story to tell in the emergency room that day!

This episode echoed the moment, fifteen years earlier, when my then-husband grabbed me by the hank of my hair and marched me, barefoot, to the emergency room. Those same words were exactly what I'd just been commanded to say to this man, as loudly as possible!

These were episodes of extreme testing to see how far I would go in this new path that I'd said yes to. In that ambulance, I was fulfilling my decision to "Go with it!" Nobody ever knew what had caused me to "flip out" that time. To the family's great relief, my sanity normalized very quickly after a few days in the hospital.

But, in spite of all that difficult obedience, there was one command I simply could not/would not obey. And that was to *"Withdraw from the Baha'i Faith!"* It was the clearest command from Above, and much easier to fulfill than any of the others. And yet, I simply couldn't! I loved that Faith too much; my loyalty ran too deep! Over all those years, I had really meant it when I vowed to remain steadfast, in spite of what anyone might do to me. They could torture me! Pull out my fingernails! I would never recant! You see, I well knew the bloody history of the early Baha'i martyrs in Iran, who did give their lives in just this way, without turning their backs on their beloved Faith.

I had never expected God, Himself, to be making that request. I didn't say no. I just didn't do anything about it. The second time that The Holy Spirit told me to withdraw, I was instructed to get a piece of paper and an envelope. This is the only time that I've ever felt automatic writing. An awkwardly-penned withdrawal sentence was addressed to the World Center of the Baha'i Faith, on Mt. Carmel in Haifa, Israel. The proper custom would have been to send my withdrawal to the Baha'i National Spiritual Assembly of the United States, in Wilmette, Illinois. But, He went right to the top with my resignation letter – because I was known and loved, by the Baha'i Universal House of Justice, for my work in the Soviet Union.

Then, my hands sealed this oddly-written letter into an envelope, which we covered messily with lots of stamps. He was taking no chances in giving me time to go to the Post Office for proper weighing and stamping. He impelled me to put the letter into the mailbox attached to the house; right beside that front porch door, witness to so many weird actions, lately. However, come dawn, I woke, free of His occupancy at that moment. *"What have I done?"* I ran downstairs, opened that screen door, snatched the as-yet-uncollected letter and tore it up on the spot! A collective groan went up within my head.

Later, after Mother died, I flew to Fairbanks, Alaska. Why, I don't recall. "More is better," meaning that farther north is even more effective/heroic/adventurous, I guess. Fairbanks was disappointing; but mostly, I remember part of the flight to get there, because of one plane-shaking incident. I was having a long conversation with "The Up" and heard this question asked of me: *"Linda Brown, what do you want to be now?"* Sincerely, I answered simply: *"All I want to be is a good Baha'i woman!"* At that very second, the small plane shuddered.

I know! I know! Air pockets! They happen all the time! But, it was mighty coincidental to that conversation.

It wasn't until 1997, two years later, that I was finally able to exile myself from the Baha'i Faith and to withdraw with willingness, and not just obedience to that command – no matter how high the Authority issuing it. I had an apartment in DeLand, Florida, living alone, where I was going through intensive and constant Inner training. Much went on, Innerly, having to do with my "mission" to defuse evil forces. That very claim, put into Outward language, makes me cringe as to the thoughts that must run through any reasonable person's mind. It sounds like a sci-fi movie plot, and in some ways, it was. I mentally created and designed in detail some Upper Institutions, such as the "Cosmic Consciousness Collection Center," or CCCC, which we then used lavishly to dispatch the negative personalities who were being sent to me, invisibly, there in the quiet privacy of that DeLand apartment.

These entities were just as puzzled as I was, to be thrown together between dimensions, and they had no idea why they'd been plopped in with me. I did know the reason, and I could hear and sense them; but I couldn't see them. Often, we chit-chatted, conversationally, to pass the time of day. We did no harm to each other, sometimes for days – until they, inevitably, became bored or impatient, and began to act up. That's when I dealt swiftly with them, by commanding them to enter my own body, un-birthing them through my female form – using my womb as the self-invented tool of elimination, the CCCC, for which I served as the portal. Every single time I followed this imaginative process, I would feel a swooshing into my lower regions, appropriate to the relative size of the entire entity. It never failed! I use the past tense here because it hardly ever happens any more. The "bullpen" must be empty!

Acting within our own authority, our symbolic solutions will literally play out upon, or perhaps in spite of, this material plane. We do manifest our sincere intentions... especially when they are enacted in harmony with the Will of God. I had been given this weird job to do; my customers were being sent to me. Therefore, *whatever* I came up with, as a way of meeting my responsibility, could be used and incorporated by Those Above, Who were counting on me to deliver on my task. By choosing to command these evil ones to go inside of myself, I theoretically risked my life every time; so instead of banishing them, I was embracing them to the utmost. That idea was even reinforced by logical reasoning on my part as I originally designed the plan. It went like this:

A negative male trying to gain dominance over any female will naturally zero in on her vagina and he will attempt rape. Okay, what if I beat him to it with a command? *"Enter my vagina, now!"* That works for me...use whatcha got! No matter that their entry is a quick, full-body shrink-down and fly-in; it's at least a tongue-in-cheek accommodation to his presumed intentions. Remember, that my body simply served as a portal to some other sphere, represented by my imagined CCCC. Inside the Cosmic Consciousness Collection Center, each one would go through several learning opportunities: sitting on a bench and looking into a positive universe, symbolized by a most attractive garden; seeing his own body crumble into dust and his consciousness encircled by a metal hoop; then, being taken to have an audience with a massive, robed God Form, Who watches benevolently as the bad boy's lifetime acts melt, like floating You-Tube videos, into a pool of water. By the time he was regretfully sentenced to have his consciousness permanently removed, the negative entity would understand exactly why his identity was being taken from him. Thus, his dollop of reasoning power would be returned to reoccupy the original stalk of itself in the mind of The Great Creative Force. Only now, it blended, anonymously, never again to be assigned to an individuated life.

I tell all in this example to illustrate to you the power of your own self-confidence, coupled with a funny, creative style of invention. Don't hold back, and don't stand on formality. Be sincere. Be unpredictable, but be "right on" in the arena of super-wacky logic if such other-worldly contests should ever be your lot.

So, that was always my sequence of disciplining these puzzled visitors. Then, another negative being would soon show up and a new mini-drama in my solo apartment would play itself out. I figured out that these were the Upline bosses of the run-of-the-mill, evil people here on Earth. My reasoning told me that those Earthly thugs would inevitably dry up when their power source disappeared from the invisible Mafia, off-planet.

At the very beginning of all this work with the Bad Boys, I realized that I mustn't use force or negative actions against them, or I'd be no better than they were. Not only were they expecting some sort of fight or rejection, but they didn't know how to cope with kindness and a lack of fear. All they knew about was war, anger and striking out against something. It didn't occur to these ghost-like forms to attack this "strange little woman" that they'd been mysteriously popped in with, because I was obviously no threat to them and they were extremely curious. However, I did need to figure out what to ultimately *do* with them when they slipped back into their tough-guy mode.

The temptation to *send them to Hell* did flit across my mind at the very first; get them out of my backyard by sending them *down* to a lower, torturous place of eternal punishment. But, I'd also been told that Earth, itself, is a Hell Realm for higher planes of existence, and it is a place of banishment for renegades of those societies. How unfair to impose our detritus on other places of living, no matter how minuscule they might be in our estimation. So, I came up with my own method of de-birthing them.

Naturally, no one in my family knew how I was spending my days, miles away in DeLand. "Certifiably insane" would have been the verdict, if I had told them. There are advantages to living single and alone – especially if you talk to the Air.

At last, I was told by The Holy Spirit, for the third time, to withdraw from the Baha'i Faith. I was ready by then! So, to underline my staunch determination to stick to my intention to obey, I dressed in my most cheerful, rose-printed sundress and my red, high-heeled shoes and then marched, painfully, the many blocks to the DeLand post office to mail my simple, hand-written, letter of resignation. A fine demonstration, of sorts! A bouquet of roses, at last, bending to His Will! No more qualms this time.

Well, by then, I was more or less self-exiled from the Faith, anyway. Basic to this was the fact that the Baha'i Teachings don't allow for psychic practices in any way, shape, or form. I personally believe that this is simply because the subject isn't dealt with in the Baha'i Writings, other than one short comment by Abdul-Baha to "leave it alone." Then, of course, there's that final line in *Gleanings*, warning that *"Should anyone arise, claiming to be a Manifestation of God within a full thousand years; that person is surely a lying impostor!"* This explains my initial horrification and disbelief at what "I thought I had heard," asked of me back in 1980. Naturally, I didn't tell the Baha'is about that – or they would have shunned me, immediately.

I realized, fifteen years later, when I had answered *"Yes!"* for the second time to that very same question, that there had to be some excellent reasons behind my mysterious Voice – even if I didn't understand what they were. So now, I was going to go with it and take my chances. Well, obviously, I couldn't walk two diverging lines. I couldn't know one thing, and espouse another. So, I went with my Inner Self, withdrew from the Baha'i Faith – and haven't looked back.

WHY DID THIS UNUSUAL EXPERIENCE HAPPEN TO ME?

Oh my Holy Spirit! What is really the story behind this call to be Your Manifestation of God?

"You might be able to help someone realize that they're not so alone as they think they are. If you can say the Unsayable. Think the Unthinkable. And, go where no one has gone before by popularizing that strange word: "Manifestationship!"

What if everyone, Innerly, had been told this very same thing and they were all scared to admit it? Linda! What if, at the end of the last Millennium, just a few years ago, God decided to tap everyone on the shoulder and ask the question: **"Will YOU be**

My Manifestation of God?" And then see what they would say. See if they are willing to be His Friend and manifest Himself, because that's where they got their consciousness from in the first place. Everyone, truly, is manifesting God, all the time, anyway, because they're connected to Him with their own brain cells. There is no other source of Mind, except that one true Source."

So! What if the real secret is the non-exclusivity of "Manifestationship?" What if everybody is getting hung up on a Station that they assume has been bestowed upon them, exclusively? And, they walk around practicing this Role, privately and only comfortably, when they are dealing with the Upper Kingdoms. But, they feel very uncomfortable when trying to face up to that Reality in their private life. What if that question is still a puzzlement and a wonderment to them?

And what if they can now simply relax and stop identifying with the ancient titles and interpretations and can realize that they have brought a title into a completely new timeframe? A completely new Millennium, where one person, one voice, is never going to have that kind of centralized Power over masses of people, ever again? We are misinterpreting that word now! That title, which used to draw all eyes unto Itself, and to call all to "Do as I do!"

We didn't notice that Dawn came up and that all people can "see with their own eyes and hear with their own ears," just as has been foretold. Wouldn't it be just like "Our Father Who Art In Heaven" to give us ALL the same birthmark, and ask us ALL to be His Manifestation of God? And then, not tell us that everyone bears that same tattoo upon their Inner Self?

It's the New Millennium! He speaks directly to us now! Each one of us can hear His Voice – and we're either too busy, or over-encrusted, to admit what's going on. Or, we simply won't talk about it when it happens. Why can't ALL of us be Manifestations of God?

Is that so hard to accept?

Yes, if we think that we're the only one!

*No, if we can admit that everyone else is too!
Could life possibly be this simple, after all?*

A FABLE – PART ONE

Here you are, a very wealthy child living on a huge estate with mansions, fields and grape arbors; surrounded by towns, businesses, and many other wonders spreading far beyond. You are a good child in a very large family consisting of a great many siblings – both naughty and nice –older and younger than yourself. Some brothers and sisters, you know; some you don't, and the same is true of your environment. The adults say that no matter how far you walk or ride, you can never reach the limits of your Father's property. You'd like to see it all and you ask lots of questions, feeling very lucky to have been born into this huge clan on such a massive estate. But, so many children!

You never see your parents, however! They're so very busy with kids running everywhere – just like you – all in great freedom. Protected by rules, of course. There's no sign of Dad, and no wonder! He has so much responsibility in order to manage this vast estate. Just to keep it going must cost a fortune!

You wish you knew the secret, but it doesn't bother you very much. You help out in every way you can: living your freeform life, thinking of your father, and wishing you knew him better. But, he's a grownup and simply terribly, terribly busy.

A FABLE – PART TWO

You are a grown-up now, yourself. Still living in the mansion on the estate. By now, you've traveled to the other properties within your Dad's domain. You've met brothers and sisters living there. Lots of them! Wow, Dad! What a passel of kids you had! What a huge family! How do you manage all this?

You've solved your loneliness, by now, in a very clever way. Missing his involvement in your life, you send him postcards.

Just put them in the mailbox addressed to: The Dad, The Boss, The Billionaire, The King, The President, Hey You! No letters to you come back – but you trust that yours get to him, just to let him know how much you love him, even if you never see him. He should be told that, especially because his work is all in behalf of this large family.

Then, one night, you're sleeping. Maybe even dreaming about your father, planning your next admiring postcard. There's a knock on your door. A servant beckons and, without a word, leads you down corridors, through tunnels, to a secret room in the heart of the castle.

There's your father! His eyes penetrate your own! ***"Will you be the inheritor of my kingdom?"***

"Yes!" comes popping from your throat before you have a chance to breathe or even to think.

He hands you a cell phone. ***"I'll call you and train you well!"***

And you are dismissed. Led back to your bed and left there by the servant. You are stunned! The only proof is the cell phone in your hand. Did you hear him right?

"The Inheritor? What does that mean? What do I do now? These lands? This house? What about the other kids? Why me? We're all his children. Why me and not them, too?" On and on.

A FABLE – PART THREE

The cell phone rings quite frequently now. You know his voice. He teaches you. He must mean business! And, life goes on. So far, the Padre hasn't died yet. He keeps calling – and now, you call back. Your postcards get longer and even more loving. You don't question his word.

"But, The Inheritor? How can I run this place, manage all these people and their children? And Why me?"

But, you don't question him. You enjoy his calls – especially, the times when he says not to worry. You'll do just fine! So, time goes by and all is well. He hasn't died yet. So, you keep quiet about all this Inheritor business. You watch the others. Some of them know so much about this property. Much more than you do.

"Why didn't Dad pick them? I don't know if I can do this, but he tells me that I'll be fine. Why me?"

You never say a word.

A FABLE – PART FOUR

But, one day, a book wants out. Wants you to publically confess that you will inherit all this. That you are The Inheritor and will carry on after Dad. This is not what you intended. To hurt their feelings. Shock them with this choice. Make them feel left out, perhaps?

You think! You cry! You face up to it! And, suddenly, there's the logic! Of course! They've ALL been called down that secret tunnel! They ALL have cell phones!

"We're ALL keeping the same secret from each other! We're ALL the "Inheritors!" We've ALL been taught our lessons! We've ALL been prepared by him to do our best! We are not alone! We stand together!

"Oh Dad, you talk to ALL of us! You love us ALL! Don't you?

YOU OLD FOX, You!

PRESENT DAY

Suffice it to say that I'm still in constant Inner connection with The Holy Spirit and other Upper Beings, and can ask questions and take dictation. What's so Schizoid about that? Let your judgment rest upon the answers I have received, as represented in these pages. Could a crazy person have invented such brief beauties? Certainly, not I...crazy or sane.

My website –www.insecretdiffusion.com – solicits cosmic questions from the public, and I post all dictated answers received on that site. Those postings comprise part of the contents of this book. My earlier book about my own cosmic questions and dictated answers was: *In Secret Diffusion: The Upper Realm Answers Questions About Earth.* My third book, *"And Yet A Little While: A Scripted Novel About Pre-Birth Planning,"* is a prequel/sequel screenplay in my Movies For The Mind Series. Both are sold on Amazon.com.

I have spent the past several years traveling solo around the world, using only my Social Security funds. Please read my first book, *"Hey Boomers, Dust Off Your Backpacks: Travel The World On A Limited Budget"* about my year-long, first-time, solo ramble around the world in 2005.

In 2012, I went around again, covering the Southern Hemisphere –and I will soon launch my longest trip yet, on my 78th birthday, to spend four years bopping about the planet. This one, I'm naming **Around The World In 80 Years,** as I will turn 80-years-old, midway through the journey, somewhere in deepest Africa. I'm creating a website and a YouTube presence titled "80 Years Per Hour" to display my videos and sage advices.

You can also follow my progress on *www.heyboomers.com* – about my life in general and my solo, hostelling and backpacking around-the-world trips. Hopefully, I will be able, throughout my travels, to become an active participant in worldwide chapters of the Hearing Voices Network as an author, speaker and good friend. Another goal is to prove that the extreme senior years are not as limited as we all seem to believe them to be. By discovering and featuring my contemporaries who are achieving wonderful and unexpected things in life, I want to inspire others to come up with their own gutsy, creative acts, full of heart and soul, for just as long as they can.

I gotta' tell 'ya, this Manifestation-business is a whole lot of fun! Come on in! The water's fine!

REFERENCES

Websites About Hearing Inner Voices:

Hearing Voices Network - www.hearing-voices.org, www.dur.ac.uk/hearingthevoice/

Email: hearingthevoice@durham.ac.uk

Hearing Voices Network, USA - www.hearingvoicesusa.org

CT Hearing Voices Network - www.cthvn.org

Wikipedia: https://en.wikipedia.org/wiki/Hearing_Voices_Network

Books About Coping With Your Pet's Death

When Your Pet Dies - by Alan D. Wolfelt, PhD

Saying Goodbye To Your Angel Animals: Finding Comfort After Losing Your Pet - by Allen Anderson and Linda Anderson

When Your Pet Dies: A Guide To Mourning, Remembering, and Healing - by Alan D. Wolfelt, PhD

The Kingdom of Heart: A Pet Loss Journal - by Patty Luckenbach, M.A., D.D.

The Land of Tears Is A Secret Place: Loss/Grief Support Journal Workbook - by Patty Luckenbach, M.A., D.D.

ABOUT THE AUTHOR

Linda J. Brown grew up in Winter Haven, Florida, and graduated with honors from the University of Florida with a degree in Journalism and Communications. She was active in campus leadership as an officer in Mortarboard, the Women's Student Association, and the University Blue Key Speaker's Bureau. She married a physician and raised two children; later becoming involved in the Citizen Diplomacy Movement after the opening of the Soviet Union. She planned and led many grassroots tours to encourage people-to-people friendship and to increase the prospects of world peace between the US and the USSR. Brown spent a total of eighteen months traveling within Russia, Ukraine and Siberia.

Brown was raised in the Episcopal Church, then spent thirty-three years as a member of the Baha'i Faith, resigning in 1997, to pursue her own inner spiritual life, once her Inner Hearing Channel opened. Her first book, **Hey Boomers, Dust Off Your Backpacks: Travel The World On A Limited Budget** tells of her adventures on the around-the-world backpacking trail as she circled the globe, alone, using only her social security income. Her continuing solo travel adventures are chronicled on Brown's website: www.heyboomers.com. In 2015, at the age of 78, she embarked upon a four-year backpacking/hosteling journey around the globe, seeking fellow Inner Voice Hearers and filming her adventures, which you may follow on YouTube under "80yearsperhour."

A second book, **In Secret Diffusion: The Upper Realm Answers Questions About Earth,** is the prequel to the one you hold in your hand. Her third book is a fictional, scripted novel: **And Yet A Little While,** which deals with pre-planning a life before reincarnation. Brown's metaphysical website is www.insecretdiffusion.com, where you are welcome to submit your own Cosmic Questions.

www.ingramcontent.com/pod-product-compliance
Lightning Source LLC
LaVergne TN
LVHW051552070426
835507LV00021B/2548